Trivial Pursuits

A comedy

Frank Vickery

Samuel French – London

New York – Sydney – Toronto – Hollywood

TRIVIAL PURSUITS

First presented at the Parc and Dare Theatre, Treorchy on 17th May 1987.

Subsequently presented at the Duke of York's Theatre, London, with the following cast of characters:

Teddy	Frank Vickery
Joyce	Christine Tuckett
Mona	Deryn Grigg
Pearl	Jackie Morgan
Roz	Iris Griffiths
Jessica	Lorraine John
Derek	Keith Warren
Nick	Mike Gray
Deidre	Lynfa Williams
Eddie	Brian Meadows

Directed by Brian Meadows

The action of the play takes place in the garden and patio area of Nick's and Roz's suburban home

ACT I   7.30 p.m. on a Saturday evening in August

ACT II   Scene 1   Later that evening
            Scene 2   Ten minutes later

Time—the present

Other titles by Frank Vickery
published by Samuel French Ltd

After I'm Gone
All's Fair
Breaking the String
Family Planning
A Night on the Tiles
A Night Out
One O'Clock from the House

ACT I

SCENE 1

The garden and patio area of Nick's and Roz's suburban home. It is 7.30 p.m. on a Saturday evening in August

Downstage is the garden area. There are one or two chairs L, a drinks table and chairs just right of C, and a long bench far R. A bit upstage is a step up to the patio area. Far L is an exit. There is a barbecue L and a swinging settee C. Immediately R and a bit behind the settee are the patio doors leading into the house, the façade of which dominates upstage. Just R of patio doors is a small table. Left of the barbecue there are windows

The Lights come up to reveal Teddy, Joyce, Mona, Pearl, Roz, Jessica and Derek. Roz is standing, the others are seated at various levels on the patio. Derek is however alone, sitting on the long bench far R. Teddy and Joyce share the swinging settee. Mona is seated in front of the drinks table. Pearl is also seated nearby, but Jessica holds herself aloof perhaps DL

A noisy game of "Charades" is in progress, with Roz "it"

Roz is shaking her head and hands "No". No one is guessing correctly. Roz sticks two fingers in the air, to indicate "second word"

Teddy And the same to you, luv!

Joyce screams with laughter at Teddy's little joke

Mona Shut up, Teddy!

Teddy and Joyce look at each other, then Teddy pulls a face. He can consider himself told off

Pearl (*continuing with the game*) Second word.

Roz puts two fingers to her arm

Mona Two syllables.

Roz gets down on all fours and mimics a cat

Teddy Lost. You've lost something.
Pearl Animal!

Roz points to Pearl, indicating she's right

   Something animal.
Mona Something something animal.

Roz shakes her head at Mona; she's on the wrong track

Joyce No, Mona—you're on the wrong track.
Teddy She's been on the wrong track for years.

Joyce and Teddy share the joke

Joyce Dog! I bet she's a dog.
Pearl (*to Roz*) Are you a dog?

Roz shakes her head "No"

Teddy She is, I used to have one like that in the back of my friend's car. (*He mimics one of those ceramic dogs with the juggling head one sees in the backs of cars*)

Joyce laughs hysterically

Mona I wish you two would stop messing about.
Teddy Oh it's only a bloody game—what's the matter with you?

Roz makes a clawing movement with one of her hands

Teddy Clawed. Claude Raines!
Mona Tiger.

Roz encourages her

Lion ... Leopard.

Roz indicates "something smaller"

Cub.
Pearl Litter!
Teddy Whipsnade.

Roz becomes increasingly agitated

Mona (*referring to Teddy*) I'm sure he does it on purpose.
Teddy I've known what it is from the start, but it's no fun if you guess it straight away.
Mona What is it, then?
Teddy She's a cat. (*To Roz*) That's what you are, aren't you? A cat?

Roz gestures that he's partly right

There you are, you see, I told you.
Pearl So it's something something cat?

Roz shakes her head

Teddy Hang on a minute now, Roz. You just said it was a cat.

Roz shakes her head, then waves her hands. She is a cat, but that's not the word she's after. Everyone is confusing her

Wait a minute ... let's get this in order. (*To Roz*) Are you a cat?

Roz nods

An ordinary house-cat?

Roz nods her head again

Is that the word—cat?

Roz shakes her head

No—right. (*To everyone*) Now are we all together on this?

Mona and Pearl ad-lib "Yes, get on with it," etc

Right, carry on then, Roz.

Roz indicates her breath

Pearl Roar!
Teddy Since when does a bloody house-cat roar!
Mona Breath.

Roz thinks Mona might be on the right track. She encourages her

Breath—breathe ...
Joyce Air ...
Mona Wind ...
Teddy Fart ...

Mona gives him a disgusted look

Joyce Food—
Pearl Whiskas—
Mona Kit-e-kat—
Teddy Paws!
Joyce (*standing triumphantly*) Mince-morsels!

Teddy drags her back down

Roz collapses in a heap on the floor

Everyone is hysterical with laughter except Mona

Eventually Roz picks herself up. She stands and eyes them wearily. She puts two fingers on her arm

Mona Second syllable.

Roz touches her ear-lobe

Teddy Sounds like.

Roz mimes playing a flute

Pearl Trumpet!
Mona Recorder?
Teddy Saxophone.
Joyce Horn. (*She goes for Teddy's privates but he fights her off*)
Mona Flute!

Roz points to her. She's got it right

Mona Flute. Sounds like flute.
Pearl Mute.
Mona Bute.
Teddy Lute.
Joyce Cute. (*She looks at Teddy*)
Teddy (*to Joyce*) Behave.
Pearl Suit.

Roz indicates she's got it

   Is it suit?

Roz nods

Mona Something something suit.

Roz puts two fingers in the air

   Second word.

Roz puts one finger on her arm

Pearl First syllable.

Roz gets down on all fours again

Teddy Oh here we go again. All right Roz, we know you're a bloody cat,
   luv.

*Roz walks around on all fours trying to mimic a cat. She stops by Pearl and
rubs her head against Pearl's arm*

Joyce What's she doing now?

Roz tries to mime a cat purring

Teddy I think she's having a funny turn.

Again Roz indicates her breath

Mona (*shouting*) Purring!

Roz jumps up—Mona's almost got it. Roz indicates "smaller"

   Purring. Purr.

Roz points to her. That's it

   Purr-suit.
Pearl (*jumping in quickly*) Trivial Pursuits!

Roz gives a great sigh of relief

Roz I thought you were never going to get it.
Pearl Right, I'm next.
Mona (*emphatically*) It ought to be me, you know. I put the two syllables
   together.
Teddy Not having a little tap, are we Mona?

Pearl A tap on the head she ought to have. (*To Mona*) Go on—you do it then.

Mona jumps to her feet and takes a little piece of paper from the drinks table

Mona (*after quickly reading it*) Right, is everyone ready?
Teddy (*getting up*) I think I'll have another drink.
Joyce (*immediately following him*) Don't forget me.
Roz I'm exhausted after that ... I think I'll have another one too.

All three move to the drinks table

Teddy Shall I cut that lemon up for you, Roz?
Mona Aren't we playing any more?
Roz Seems to have come to a natural end, Mona.
Teddy (*almost under his breath*) Pity she wouldn't come to a natural end.
Joyce Yeah. (*To Mona*) We'll have a game of hang-man after, luv.
Mona Trust it to finish on my turn.
Roz Never mind ... maybe we'll play something else later.
Mona (*turning to Jessica*) Jessica, would you like to play?

Jessica doesn't answer, she just laughs as she chews on her gum and heads for the house

Roz (*to Jessica as she passes*) Would you like another drink, dear?
Jessica No thanks ... not yet.

Jessica exits

Roz, Teddy and Joyce busy themselves at the drinks table

Mona takes Pearl DR *to have a confidential chat*

Mona Funny girl.
Pearl She's very pretty. I imagine she'll look good on stage.
Mona Which is probably why Nick involved her. She can't sing you know. I've heard her. Where did he get her from I wonder.
Pearl I think he spotted her in a church pantomime. (*She hands Mona a cigarette*)

The action goes back to the drinks table

Roz (*to Joyce*) I think it should be straight lemonade for you.
Joyce Oh, don't be like that, Roz.
Roz You're supposed to be on the wagon.
Joyce I am ... but I have been known to fall off occasionally.
Roz I'll just put in a dash of Martini, then.
Teddy Yes, go on—just a dash.

Roz begins to fill the glass when Teddy pretends to accidentally touch the bottom of the bottle, which results in Joyce having a much larger measure than Roz intended

Roz (*sarcastically*) Oh, thank you very much, Teddy.

Teddy and Joyce smile and wink at each other

Immediately Joyce gets her drink she takes it, still laughing DR *towards Derek, who is still sitting alone on the bench. Seeing him she laughs even louder and does an immediate about-turn straight back to the drinks table*

Roz Gin for you, Teddy?
Teddy Yes, please, ice and lemon.

Mona, hearing this, decides to butt in

Mona I'm not being funny, Roz, but I've been waiting longer than him.
Roz You've hardly been waiting at all, Mona.
Mona I hate people who cheat their turn.
Teddy You just hate people, luv.
Mona (*to Pearl*) He's always the same.
Roz Why don't you two try and get on? You'll be making me feel sorry I invited you both.
Mona It's him, it is. He's forever making fun of me.
Teddy You are forever giving me the opportunity. (*He takes his drink from Roz*) Thanks, luv.
Pearl (*to Mona*) I remember a time when you two were very close.
Mona No, I don't think so.
Roz Oh yes you were, Mona. When you first joined the society you were quite smitten by our Teddy.

Roz takes drinks over to Mona and Pearl

Mona (*put out*) When I first joined the society I was very friendly with everyone. Well you are, aren't you? It's after you've been there a few months—or as in my case a few years—that you really find out who your friends are!

Mona takes her drink and storms past Roz and goes immediately indoors

Teddy and Joyce look at each other. Teddy then turns to see Mona disappearing through the patio doors. He turns back to Joyce

Teddy
Joyce (*together*) Ooohhh!

They burst into laughter, joined by Roz and Pearl. Roz and Pearl move DR *leaving Teddy and Joyce* C. *They return to the settee and sit down*

Teddy (*calming himself down*) Listen, Joyce—I knew I wanted to ask you something. Have you heard any more news?
Joyce About what?
Teddy About the next production?
Joyce Well I've heard definitely that it's five different shows in the last week.
Teddy I've heard, from someone in Pearl's Tupperware-party—
Joyce Roz?
Teddy I can't say . . . that it's *Hello Dolly*.

Joyce Never!

Teddy It's what I've heard. Mind you, I've also heard *Camelot, Cabaret, Seven Brides* and, (*he takes on a Scottish accent*) *Brigadoon*. What have you heard?

Joyce I've heard it's *Half a Sixpence*—

Teddy makes a face

Guys and Dolls—

Teddy makes an even bigger face

Finian's Rainbow—

Teddy puts his hands on his chest as if he's just belched and has a very nasty taste in his mouth

—and *Mame*.

Teddy (*gobsmacked*) *Mame!*

Joyce Can you see me as Mame, Ted? (*She begins to sing a line from the show, swinging her leg, which rests on the arm of the chair, in time to the music*) "Light my candle ..."

Teddy No luv, you're more of a Vera Charles.

Joyce But she's a drunk.

Teddy (*reaching for his gin and tonic*) Yes, that's right. That's only four. You said you heard five.

Joyce That's right. Now what was the other one? (*She pauses*) Oh, yes, I know ... *Phantom of the Opera*.

Teddy Oh, hey (*putting a hand over one side of his face, he starts to sing*) "Say you'll stay with me each night ...

Joyce joins in

Joyce⎱
Teddy⎰ (*together*) "... each morning ..."

Joyce A bloody mask you ought to have, luv. (*She helps herself to another drink*)

Teddy It's any bugger's guess, then.

During the next dialogue Teddy lights a cigarette

Pearl I was hoping to have a quiet word with him.

Roz There's no need to see him in the garage. It's full of stage furniture anyway. He's been painting a lot of benches white. They're probably still wet, he only did them this afternoon. Take him into the lounge. Nobody'll bother you there.

Pearl What it is, you see ... he's planning to announce the next show tonight, and I wanted to make it clear to him the exact state of the group's bank balance. I've got to make him realize that there are a lot of shows we just can't afford to put on. God forbid—we still owe bills from our last fiasco. Between me and you we've got big problems, Roz. If Nick doesn't choose a show that's box office, next year there's not going to be a Trealaw and District Operatic Society.

Roz It's that bad?

Pearl We still owe the orchestra seven hundred and fifty pounds, and I think we should settle those kind of bills before we go into another production.

Roz Better leave Nick to me, Pearl. Maybe I can get through to him better than you.

Roz and Pearl move to join Teddy and Joyce

Joyce (*standing up, holding an empty glass; calling*) Derek?

Derek looks over at her

Drinkie?

Derek holds up his hand, waves it slightly and shakes his head. He even manages a self-pitying smile

Roz Oh . . . pity to leave him all over there on his own.

Pearl Yeah, Teddy go and have a word with him.

Teddy You bugger off . . .

Joyce Yes, go on. We'll come over and join you after.

Joyce and Pearl pull Teddy to his feet and push him in Derek's direction

Teddy Why me? You always send me to do the bloody shit.

Pearl and Joyce give him one final push and Teddy is almost at the bench. Derek looks up at him. Teddy looks back at the three women who are all smiling and waving the backs of their hands, encouraging him to go nearer

Teddy takes a deep breath, realizing he's been pushed too far to make an acceptable retreat. He has no choice but to join Derek

Teddy (*with false enthusiasm*) Hello Derek. How's it going kid? All right?

He sits next to Derek on the bench and crosses his legs. He holds his cigarettes in one hand and his gin and tonic in the other

Derek takes one look at him and after a brief moment bursts into tears. Teddy can't believe his eyes. He turns around to look in complete amazement at the women. They still encourage him to continue

(*Not really sure how to proceed*) Oh come on now, Derek. Can't be as bad as all that, whatever it is.

Derek (*still emotional but trying to pull himself together*) I'm sorry. I'm sorry, Teddy. (*After a slight thought*) It is Teddy, isn't it?

Teddy is exhaling his cigarette as he nods to confirm

Yes. I wish I hadn't done that . . . it's so embarrassing.

Teddy I don't know why you don't have a drink.

Derek (*with great importance*) Do you know what the day after tomorrow is? (*He raises his voice*) Have you got any idea what day it is the day after tomorrow?

Teddy (*after a brief mental check*) Monday, Derek.

Derek (*shouting*) Monday! Monday August the twenty-first.

Teddy looks back towards the women hoping they might be able to help him understand the significance. They don't understand it either. Teddy turns back to Derek

Teddy Special, is it? Birthday or something?
Derek It's "D" day, Teddy. It's the beginning of the end.

Teddy looks back to Joyce, who holds up four fingers

Teddy (*turning back to Derek*) Oh, so you'll be forty . . . well, there's nothing wrong in that.
Derek (*suddenly very confidential but still intense*) You know that Deidre and I have separated?
Teddy Well yes . . . you can't belong to an amateur operatic society and not get to hear something like that.
Derek The decree absolute comes through on Monday. After that there's nothing. Finished. Seventeen years down the drain. It's a long time. And I had no idea, you see.
Teddy Never. (*He looks back to the women and mouths for them to hurry up and join him*)

Joyce moves to the drinks table to mix Derek a drink

Derek As far as I knew everything was fine. I didn't suspect a thing. She'd gone for a week before I knew she was missing. If I hadn't run out of shirts I never would have found out.

Joyce and Pearl join them

Roz tries unsuccessfully to light the barbecue

Joyce (*moving round the back of the bench to arrive on Derek's left*) Here you are, Derek. I've brought you a drink anyway.

Pearl sits on the arm of the bench, on Teddy's right

Derek (*taking the drink*) I haven't been out for months. (*He pauses*) Haven't seen Deidre since I don't know when. And that helps in a funny sort of way. I'd give anything to see her, but I know I'm all right as long as I don't.

All three look at each other

Not that we'd quarrel or anything like that if we did meet. It's just that I know I'd get terribly upset. (*To Joyce*) My whole world collapsed when she left, you see.

All three look out, not sure where to position their eyes

Derek continues with renewed volume

I thought everyone had forgot about me. Then yesterday the phone rings and it's Roz.

All three raise their glasses in a sarcastic toast to Roz, who is still busy with the barbecue

Teddy
Joyce } *(together)* Good old Roz.
Pearl

Derek Nick ought to put her in a show, you know. Her timing is absolutely impeccable. That phone call saved my life. (*He pauses*) I can tell you three because I know it won't go any further ...

Joyce almost chokes

All three move closer to Derek

The fact is ... I've been absolutely desperate since Deidre left.

Joyce takes full advantage of the remark, putting her arm around his neck making an obvious play for him. Derek doesn't know what hit him. Teddy comes to his rescue, managing to push Joyce off

Teddy (*pushing Joyce away*) Hey no, Derek ... you shouldn't say things like that in front of Joyce.

Derek (*trying to put the misunderstanding right*) No, I don't mean desperate for a woman. I've never been desperate for that.

Teddy Oh, nor me. (*He slips his left hand on to Derek's knee*)

Derek (*immediately replacing Teddy's hand*) No, I mean desperate for Deidre. (*He pauses*) I couldn't see any point in going on. I've been staying in work till all hours. Nothing to go home for. Mind you, business is booming ... full books ... doubled the orders. Money's rolling in ... but what's the point without—

Teddy
Joyce } (*together*)—Deidre.
Pearl

Derek Exactly. I come home to an empty house—no meal ready, I'm in bed by nine.

Joyce and Teddy share a look

I've even seriously thought—well more than thought about ... you know. (*Hinting suicide*). I even decided how I was going to do it.

Joyce Tablets are the best way.

Derek I know ... but would you believe it? ... I went to the bathroom cabinet and I didn't even have a bloody aspirin. All I could find was half a bottle of Deidre's water tablets.

Pearl (*really concerned*) I hope you didn't take them, Derek.

Teddy Yeah, or you'd have pissed yourself to death.

Joyce and Teddy almost collapse with laughter. Pearl nudges Teddy

Derek I decided to jump in the end.

Joyce (*tagged on the end of her laugh*) What changed your bloody mind?

Teddy Thought better of it in the nick of time, I suppose.

Derek No, not really. I had all the paintwork done the week before ...

thought I'd entice Deidre back that way, but it didn't work. Well, you know how it is . . . I couldn't get the window open. Still can't. Banged on it with my fist a couple of times and ended up spraining my wrist. By the time I went for a crêpe bandage . . . I'd gone off the idea.

Teddy (*to the women*) Mind you, he wouldn't have damaged much more than his wrist if he *had* jumped. He lives in a bungalow.

Derek It is a *dormer*.

Pearl You didn't really want to commit suicide, Derek. It was a cry for help.

Derek I suppose you're right. It is help I need. That's why it's wonderful to have friends like you. It's not going to be easy for me, but some say I'll be all right after Monday. (*To the women*) That's when the decree absolute comes through. (*He begins to get upset*) That's when it'll all be . . .

Teddy (*scornfully*) Derek!

Derek immediately pulls himself together

Joyce Are you going to have a little drink up, Derek? A celebration? I'll come if you are.

Derek I won't be in any mood to celebrate, Joyce. (*After a quick mental check*) It *is* Joyce, isn't it?

Joyce Yes, luv.

Derek Yes, that's right. I know most men in my position would. Celebrate, I mean. I know half a dozen in work who'd change places with me tomorrow. Well, Monday anyway. But it's not like that for me. You see, I still love my wife.

Mona enters and stands just outside the patio doors. She turns to Roz, who is still at the barbecue

Mona (*to Roz*) Roz, you really ought to do something about that girl.

Roz What girl?

Mona That Jessica. You distinctly heard me say I needed to use the bathroom—

Roz Did I?

Mona Well, she sneaked up behind my back and nipped in before me.

Roz What's the matter with the downstairs bathroom?

Mona You have a bathroom downstairs as well?

Roz nods

Well! Why didn't someone say?

Mona exits hurriedly back into the house

Derek is still prattling on. The others are all sitting round looking positively bored out of their skulls

Derek I can't tell you how good it feels to be wanted. Since Deidre and I separated I don't get invited anywhere. They still invite her, of course, but on the whole people tend to forget about me. (*He realizes he hasn't got their attention. He repeats what he has just said a little louder*) I say on the whole people tend to forget about me. But not you ... not you lot. True friends.

Roz giving up on the barbecue, comes over to join them

Ah ... there she is. I was just saying, Roz ... since Deidre and I—
Roz (*sharply*) Yes. (*A little more politely*) I heard.

There is a pause

Derek I thought there would have been more here than this, Roz.

Pearl, Joyce and Teddy look up at Roz. She looks guilty

Roz No ... no, this is about it.
Joyce We thought you might have brought someone, didn't we, Roz?
Derek No—I've finished with women. I'll never give my heart to another woman.
Roz We thought you might have brought Tessa, your secretary.
Derek Tessa? Oh no ... no, no. She's been very good to me, mind. Very kind. But no one could ever take the place of Deidre.

During the following the three women quietly move way, leaving Derek alone with Teddy. They take up a position towards the back, right of the barbecue. They watch the proceedings from that distance

It's all such a terrible shame, isn't it? You know of course about the decree absolute? Monday. Day after tomorrow. I'm still quite numbed by it all. Speechless, really. My brain can't seem to accept the final blow. I'll never understand it ... well, her. I'll never understand her. Now there's a woman who had everything. A Zanussi dishwasher ... Toshiba microwave ... Tower slo-cooker ... Moulinex blender ... a Pifco something or other ... I don't know what she used that for. Everything she had.

Teddy turns to react to Pearl, only to find she isn't there. Then he looks and realizes that the others have deserted him too. He looks and finds them at the back of the patio. He looks back at Derek who is still rabbiting on, then carefully sneaks away to join the others. Derek continues

Do you know what I said to her once? "Let's go on a world cruise," I said. And do you know what she said to me? As God is my judge, she said, "Oh, I don't know. I'd rather go somewhere else." Everything that woman had. Everything. And she hasn't even thrown it away for another man. Mind you, I'm glad about that. I'm bad enough as it is. I'm sure I wouldn't be able to cope if there was a third par—

He suddenly becomes aware that he is on his own. He looks around and sees the others are beginning their own conversation. He cries silently

Joyce (*trying to whisper*) Well, who's going to tell him?
Teddy (*also keeping his voice down*) I'd leave it if I were you. He'll know soon enough when she arrives.
Roz And just think what could happen then. Maybe it's better if he's told now, then he might decide to leave.

Teddy Derek and Deidre in the same company . . .

Roz (*to Joyce*) It was silly of you to ask her.

Joyce Well, I didn't know you were going to ask Derek.

Roz I felt sorry for him.

Joyce Anyway, I thought it was quite a friendly separation. I didn't realize until he was going just now how much he's still involved with her . . . or wants to be.

Teddy (*looking at his watch*) It's getting late. Maybe she's not coming.

Joyce She said she wouldn't be early. You know her mother's in hospital.

Teddy (*nodding*) Hysterectomy.

Joyce She's probably coming on here afterwards.

Teddy Hey, listen, I've got an idea. Let's get him drunk. He might pass out and be none the wiser.

Joyce Now that's a good idea.

Roz Yes, there's something in that.

Teddy Right, well, who's prepared now then to go down and take him a drink?

They all turn away. No one is prepared to risk another encounter

(*Sighing*) Well, that knocks that on the head!

Mona comes out of the house

Mona Ah . . . that's better.

Teddy, Joyce, Roz and Pearl exchange a look. They all have the same thought

Roz (*quickly pouring a drink*) Mona . . . take a drink down to Derek, will you?

Mona (*handing Roz her empty glass*) I may as well have another one as well. (*Slight pause*) I love your bathroom.

Roz Do you?

Mona Very nice. I could live in there. It's almost as big as my flat. You've got lovely taste.

Roz Thank you.

Mona I'm surprised. The way you've got the carpet going up the side of the bath . . . it gives it that lovely look of opulence.

Roz It's only Tumble-Twist.

Mona I wish I could have it in my bathroom, but of course I haven't got a bath . . . and it wouldn't have the same effect, would it, going up the side of the shower base? Toilet's knacky, too.

Teddy (*stepping forward slightly to join the conversation*) Knacky?

Mona Yes . . . it's synphonic. Nick was telling me earlier on. I'll be honest with you, I wasn't sure what synphonic meant—I'm still not, really. As I touched the handle I half expected it to play something from *South Pacific*.

Teddy (*moving even closer to Mona*) It means . . . it sucks instead of flushes.

At this point Joyce slips up close to Teddy and touches and tickles his backside as she moves behind

Teddy gives a little scream, then laughs

Roz hands Mona hers and Derek's drink

Joyce helps herself to whatever she wants from the table. Teddy gently pushes Mona off in Derek's direction

(*To Mona*) Off you go.

They all gather to watch as Mona approaches Derek

Mona Derek?

Derek looks at her and she hands him his drink

Derek Oh ... Mona. Thank you very much.

She sits next to him on the bench

(*After making a quick mental check*) It is Mona, isn't it?

She nods

I was far away then. Off on another planet.
Mona Thinking about work?
Derek No, about Deidre actually.

The others turn away at this point. They are exasperated. They know exactly what is coming. Joyce and Teddy move to sit on the swinging settee. Joyce immediately shows him the bottle of vodka she has managed to smuggle past Roz

Nick comes out of the house. He moves to join Roz and Pearl

Roz (*seeing him*) There you are! I was beginning to wonder what had happened to you. Did you have any luck?
Nick All I could find was one miserly fire-lighter—and that feels as dry as a cork.
Roz Are you going to have a go?
Nick I've got nothing else to do.

Nick goes to the barbecue. After moving the charcoal he places the fire-lighter. Roz winks at Pearl and gestures for her to leave them alone together

Pearl gets the message and immediately moves towards Derek and Mona, then stops. She turns to Teddy and Joyce, who are giggling on the settee. She can't join them either

Pearl exits, going indoors

Roz I think we should have bought an electric one.
Nick Food doesn't taste the same.
Roz Do you think that's going to do the trick?
Nick If it isn't I'm going to try half a gallon of petrol.

Roz spots something about Nick

Roz Nick, what have you done?

He looks at her, not understanding

Turn around.

He does

You're covered in paint.

Nick What?

Roz You are, all down one side.

He turns to try and see for himself and the audience sees that he has two or three stripes of white paint down one side of his shirt and trousers

Nick Oh, shit!

Roz How did you manage that?

Nick (*embarrassed*) I forgot I'd painted the bloody things, didn't I? I would have thought they'd be dry by now.

Roz You look for all the world as if you've been lying down.

Nick (*trying to laugh it off*) Don't be silly.

There is an awkward pause between them

Give me the matches.

She does

Here goes.

He tries several times to light the barbecue but he can't get it going. Every attempt he makes is making him more and more bad-tempered, until in the end he slings the matches across the patio

Derek When do you think is the worst time? Go on, put yourself in my position and have a guess at when I miss her most.

Mona (*not wanting this conversation*) I've no idea, Derek.

Derek Have a guess.

Mona (*anything to shut him up*) Meal times?

Derek No.

Mona Bed times?

Derek No.

Mona (*getting very impatient*) In the mornings!

Derek Try again.

Mona gets up without answering and walks around to the back of the bench

Roz Looks like petrol is the answer then.

Nick sits down, obviously fed up with the situation

Stay there, I'll get you a drink. (*She goes to the drinks table*) I can see me having to freeze all the steak.

Nick (*looking at the barbecue and shaking his head*) It's not the actual barbecue, it can't be.

Roz Perhaps it's got something to do with the weather. It hasn't been a wonderful day. Maybe there's a lot of dampness in the air.

Nick More likely the cat's pissed on the charcoal.

Throughout Mona and Derek's exchange, Nick has several more attempts at lighting the fire, without success

Mona (*at the end of her tether*) All right Derek, I give up.

Derek One more guess.

Mona (*almost spitting*) Nine o'clock.

Derek (*excitedly*) No.

Mona Derek, I don't want to know and to be honest I really don't care, but if you don't tell me soon I swear I'm going to do something I'm sure we'll both regret.

Derek (*triumphantly*) Ten past three!

Mona Ten past three?

Derek In the morning. I turn over in bed, fart, and apologize to the duvet.

The action shifts back to Nick

Nick Well that's it—I've had enough. (*He sits down and finishes his drink*)

Roz sits next to him

Roz Maybe we could take it indoors and start it off in there.

Nick shakes his head

Pause

    Nick ... about the next production—

Nick Don't ask me to tell you what it is, Roz. I don't tell anyone, you know that.

Roz (*huffily*) I wasn't going to. (*Pause*) I was going to talk to you about— (*She nods in Teddy's and Joyce's direction*)

Nick Who?

Roz nods again

    Teddy?

Roz Joyce. You are going to look after her, aren't you? I mean you did half-promise me you'd give her something in the next show.

Nick I didn't do any such thing.

During the following speech Teddy and Joyce stop chatting and, without looking round, listen in

Roz (*insisting*) You did. You were talking about it a fortnight ago. There was a strong rumour going round that you were going to do *Oklahoma*, and when I asked you about it you said, as you always do, that you couldn't confirm anything, but you also said that if you were doing *Oklahoma*, Joyce would be a strong contender for Laurie.

Joyce is over the moon. She would be thrilled to play the lead

Nick You didn't tell her I said that, did you?

Joyce and Teddy mime a very excited conversation

Roz Of course I didn't. I couldn't build her up and chance letting her down, she'd never be able to take it. Not after the last episode. Her confidence is rock-bottom, Nick. I mean, she's my sister and I don't like to see her like that. (*Slight pause*) When do you plan to announce it?

Nick (*looking at his watch*) Not for about an hour.

He smiles cheekily at her before clapping his hands together and moving towards Teddy and Joyce

Slight problem, I'm afraid. No barbecue tonight.

Teddy (*outraged*) What?

Joyce (*now more progressively drunk*) What's the matter? Can't light it?

Nick I've tried everything.

Joyce Just a minute. You've got a barbecue, haven't you, Ted?

Teddy Yes.

Joyce Well, how do you manage?

Teddy It's easy—I plug it in.

Joyce and Teddy laugh together

Nick I've tried a fire-lighter, nothing seems to work.

Teddy I remember my mother trying to light the fire, years ago now of course, before we had the gas. She used to throw sugar on it.

Nick Sugar?

Teddy Yeah, and if that didn't work she used to chuck me on.

Joyce is laughing helplessly

Nick (*as a last resort*) You wouldn't have a bash, would you Teddy? (*He turns away from Teddy but bends down in front of him, still fiddling with the barbecue*) You might have more luck than me.

Teddy hands Joyce his glass. She immediately drinks out of it

Teddy Yes, I don't mind. I'll have a go. (*Looking at Nick's backside before he makes another move*) You know me . . . I'll have a bash at anything.

Nick and Teddy fuss with the barbecue, leaving Joyce alone on the settee. Roz takes a refill down to Derek and Mona

Derek (*to Roz*) Oh, I don't know if I should have any more.

Roz Oh, come on, Derek, the night is young.

Derek (*putting his hand to his head*) I don't feel altogether here.

Mona (*alarmed*) You're not going to be ill, are you?

Derek No, no, it's just that I'm not sure if I've had one too many already.

Roz You're not driving, are you?

Derek No.

Roz (*giving him the drink*) Well, enjoy yourself then.

Joyce (*calling*) Roz?

Roz looks over at Joyce

Can I have a word?

By this time Teddy has given up on the barbecue too. He has managed to light a cigarette for himself, though

Teddy No ... I think you've got a problem there, Nick.

Roz (*to Mona and Derek*) Excuse me.

Teddy It's a bit late now of course, but you know what the answer is, don't you?

Roz joins Joyce on the settee

Joyce I don't want you for anything. I just thought you needed rescuing.

Nick (*to Teddy*) No, what?

Teddy You should have invited Damien here.

Nick Who?

Teddy Damien. Damien Townsend. You remember him. He did the Artful Dodger for us about ... oh, about six years ago.

Nick What has he got to do with lighting the barbecue?

Teddy Well not many people know this ... but he's just done two years for arson.

Nick I thought he was in drama school.

Teddy He was. He burnt it down. But I don't believe he ever went there. I reckon it was a ruse put round by his mother. Mind you, he was an even bigger embarrassment to his father. While his father was being honoured for twenty-five years in the fire service, Damien was busy setting light to a bus shelter in Cymmer.

Teddy and Nick sit on the step just behind the barbecue. Joyce has become very emotional, and is breaking down in front of Roz

Joyce (*quietly screaming*) Rozzzzzz! I'm desperate. I don't care if it *is* bloody *Oklahoma*, as long as I'm in it.

Roz Come on ... pull yourself together. I've told you ... leave everything to me.

Joyce See, Laurie doesn't have to be young. And surely it would depend largely on the age of Curly. I mean, you can hardly have an eighteen-year-old Laurie if your Curly will be forty next June. (*Slight pause*) If it ... is *Oklahoma*, I wonder who he has in mind for Curly?

Teddy (*to Nick*) Did I tell you I've been asked to play Schubert in *Lilac Time*?

Nick Yes.

Teddy Trouble is it's coming off a fortnight before ours. (*Slight pause*) I haven't given them my answer yet—though somebody rings me every day. "No, I can't give you my answer yet," I say—"cause I've still got to find out what my other commitments are." Well I have, haven't I?

Nick doesn't answer

Of course my loyalty is with our company. (*He pauses*) I mean, I want to play Schubert, don't get me wrong, but I'd much prefer to be in our next production. (*He takes a long drag on his cigarette then blows it out*) Whatever it is. (*He sneaks a look over at Nick, who is looking dead ahead, nodding slowly, not really committing himself*)

Pearl comes to the patio window and peers out. She sees that Roz is not now with Nick, and comes back into the garden

Pearl pours herself a drink before walking down to CS

Derek (*by now a little tiddly*) So that's why everyone's here. To find out the next show.

Mona That's right.

Derek Is there anything in particular you want to do?

Mona I don't really mind whatever it is—but there'd better be some good dancing numbers in it.

Derek Dancing?

Mona Yes. (*She pauses*) I'm Mona Middleton. (*She pauses*) Company choreographer.

Derek Oh I see. (*He pauses*) Bit of a dancer then, are you?

Mona (*at full fettle*) I *create*! The others dance.

Derek Would you like to do a bit for me here now?

Mona (*outraged*) Certainly not!

Derek Fair enough.

Pearl joins them

Teddy (*scheming*) Seen anything of your mother lately, Nick?

Nick Not this week, no.

Teddy Ohhhhh, she loves it there, you know. Going into sheltered accommodation is the best thing that's happened to her.

Nick She was kicking and screaming going in.

Teddy Her words ... not mine. (*He pauses*) Yes, she's very happy there, Nick.

Nick I'm glad.

Teddy Couldn't stop thanking me. Got quite embarrassing in the end.

Nick That's my mother.

Teddy It's not you who should be thanking me, I said. It's that son of yours—that Nick, I said. It's him I pulled the strings for.

Nick smiles uncomfortably. Teddy slips one hand under Nick's arm and leads him DS

Mind you, I regretted saying that afterwards. I mean if it got back to my superiors in housing that I worked a flanker for a friend—well, it would mean the chop for me. And I don't mean a vasectomy, either.

There's a slight pause. Nick takes Teddy's glass and goes to the table to refill it. Teddy follows close behind

Mona (*to Pearl, outraged*) I wasn't aware of that.

Pearl Not many people are. I should never have told you. You won't let it go any further, will you?

Mona Well, I don't know. I think people should know. I was under the impression that the company had plenty of money.

Pearl No, we're in the red, believe me.

Teddy (*to Nick*) I had to see her yesterday—your mother, that is—on a professional matter.

Nick Ice and lemon?

Teddy Please. Our department had a complaint about her from her warden.
   They sent me there to deal with it.
Nick What's the problem? Hasn't she been behaving herself?
Teddy Well . . . no.
Nick I thought she was settling in fine. She told me she made a lot of
   friends.
Teddy Yes. That's the problem.
Nick (*handing Teddy the drink*) I'm not altogether with you, Teddy.
Teddy (*taking Nick's arm and leading him* DR) Mrs Hall—the warden—
   won't have it—and it upsets the other residents.
Nick What exactly has she done?
Teddy She makes friends.
Nick (*relieved*) Is that all?
Teddy With men. She invites them to her flat for tea . . . and supper. The
   warden did her morning round last Thursday and found one had stayed
   for breakfast. She's the talk of the place and she's only been there a
   fortnight.
Nick Did you speak to her about it?
Teddy Well, yes.
Nick What did she say?
Teddy She said that he'd only that minute popped in.
Nick What were they doing when the warden called?
Teddy Drinking tea.
Nick Well, there's no harm in that.
Teddy In bed!
Nick (*shocked*) Dear God!
Teddy It's right enough, Nick. Apparently it happened three times the first
   week.
Nick Three times? He's practically living there.
Teddy Oooh, hey, it's not always the same man.

Nick retreats to the drinks table. Teddy follows immediately

Joyce I hope you haven't been pulling any strings with Nick, Roz.
Roz What do you mean?
Joyce Well, I hope he's not going to give me a part just because you're my
   sister. If I'm going to be involved in the next show, I want it to be on my
   own merits. Mind you, in that case I'll be lucky to get a walk-on.
Roz He's not going to hold last year's show against you.
Joyce Oh, I hope not. I still get embarrassed thinking about it.
Roz I've told you, you've got to put all that behind you.
Joyce That's right. I've got to go out there and give it hell!
Nick What are you going to do about it?
Teddy Well, luckily the warden complained to me personally, so hopefully
   we can sort it out between ourselves. If the authorities got to know
   officially, there's no doubt about it—she'd be out on her arse.
Nick Evicted?
Teddy Oh, yes. And before you know it she'd be back here with you.
Nick We've got to sort things out, Teddy. We've got to put things right.

Teddy (*moving to put out his cigarette in the ash-tray on the table*) I've done all I can, Nick. It's up to you to talk to her now.

Nick I will. I'll have a word tomorrow.

Teddy I'll do what I can as far as the office is concerned of course, but we can only turn a blind eye for so long.

Nick I'm very grateful to you, Teddy.

Teddy freezes immediately. This is exactly what he's been waiting to hear

Teddy Are you?

Nick Yes—very grateful indeed. If ever there's anything I can do for you ...

Teddy Well, funny enough there is, luv ... yes. (*Leading him* DR *again*) The thing is, see ... I'll be forty next June.

Nick (*after a slight pause*) Yes?

Teddy If I don't get to play Curly this year, I'm going to be too old.

Nick Curly?

Teddy Yes. *Oklahoma.*

Nick (*now realizing exactly what Teddy is after*) Teddy, the show's been chosen.

Teddy Hey now, look, it's not going to be easy keeping your mother's behaviour under wraps.

Nick You're putting me in a bit of a spot, Teddy.

Teddy Hey listen luv, your mother's putting me in a bloody big hole!

Nick Teddy ... next year. I'll do it next year.

Teddy (*determined*) *Now*, Nick. It's got to be *now*. And while we're at it— what about ... Joyce? (*He nods over in her direction*)

Roz isn't coping very well with Joyce and has just decided to take her indoors

Nick What about her?

Teddy You'll have to find something for her as well.

Nick Hang on now, look, Teddy—

Teddy She's got a lot riding on this one—Joyce. Got a lot to prove, hasn't she?

Nick doesn't answer

And not just to herself—to the audience as well. I mean she felt so bad after her disaster in *Calamity Jane*, didn't she? *Calamity Jane*? She did the right show—a bloody calamity it was.

Roz comes back out of the house

Nick (*not really wanting to hear this*) Yes, all right Teddy.

Teddy And I mean, poor bugger, what can you say to her after something like that?

Roz comes to stand in between them at this point

Don't worry, luv, I'm sure the audience didn't notice? The audience were bloody hysterical. Mind you, she made it worse by going through with it, the silly old cow.

Roz is about to open her mouth to defend Joyce when Teddy realizes what he's said and to whom he's said it and tries to rescue himself

But that's nerves, that is. Hell of a thing, nerves. (*Slight pause. For Nick's benefit*) And I don't care what anybody says I reckon she should have taken a curtain-call regardless. I mean when you go and see *Calamity Jane* you expect to see Calam in the line-up. Poor old Jeff had to take the curtain-call on his own. (*He pauses*) Yes, she's got a lot riding on this one, Joyce. So I think you should cast her in *Oklahoma* as well.

Nick She's hardly a Laurie.

Teddy (*panicking*) Bloody hell, no! I wasn't thinking of Laurie. Give her Aunt Eller. God knows that's big enough for her after Calam. Nice little character part—no solo singing—not a lot of make-up—a few verses of *Oklahoma*—she'll be bloody marvellous. What do you say?

Nick (*taking a deep breath; he's trapped*) Leave it to me. I'll sort something out.

Teddy (*overjoyed*) Oh thank you, Nick. And remember what I said ... it'll be to your advantage as well. (*He winks at him*) You know what I mean, don't you? (*He touches his nose with his forefinger*)

Teddy moves away to join the others, with Roz hanging on to his arm

(*Singing*) "Oh what a beautiful morning ..." Hey, listen, girls, have I got news for you!

Roz gestures for him not to say anything. The others ad-lib trying to get him to spill the beans

Nick tries to get some sort of order

Nick Listen, everyone. Listen. Slight problem ... well, big problem really. There's definitely no barbecue tonight.

Mona (*outraged*) What?

Nick Sorry. Impossible to light the bloody thing.

Roz No, wait a minute ... don't give up yet. (*Going to the barbecue*) Leave it to me. Teddy, will you give me a hand?

Teddy (*joining her*) Yes, what do you want, luv?

Roz (*to Nick*) Give me half an hour—I've got an idea. (*To Teddy*) Carry this in with me, Ted?

Teddy You leave that where it is. I'll carry it on my own. (*He picks it up and heads for the house*)

Roz Are you sure?

Teddy Yes, I'll manage it ... you know me, I'm all man.

Teddy exits with Roz following him indoors

Nick (*to Roz as she passes behind him*) I hope you know what you're doing. (*He goes and pours himself another drink*) Any more drinks, anyone?

Pearl takes this opportunity to speak to Nick, taking him over towards the settee

Pearl Nick, about the next show—

Nick Oh Pearl, don't start on me now, I don't think I could handle it.

Pearl *You* can't handle it? You don't know what I've got to put up with. Did Roz tell you? It's getting so bad I'm afraid to go out. (*She goes into her handbag, takes out a handful of papers, and holds them out to Nick*)

Nick What are those?

Pearl Bills, Nick. Outstanding bills. Harry Crossman, the printer, won't even speak to me now.

Nick Well I don't see why we should pay him two hundred and fifty pounds for programmes that didn't arrive until the Wednesday the week of the show. The ink was still wet on the Saturday. He left an *E* out of "Jane", which I'm sure is part of the reason people stayed away in droves. I mean, who the hell has heard of the musical *Calamity Jan*?

Pearl And then there's the orchestra.

Nick We've paid the orchestra.

Pearl There's still seven hundred and fifty pounds outstanding. If you don't pay up you're not going to have them for the next production.

Nick How much money have we got in the bank?

Pearl The account is about three thousand pounds —

Nick (*jumping in*) Well, that's enough to get one with.

Pearl —overdrawn.

Nick Overdrawn?

Pearl nods

You mean there's nothing there?

Pearl Luckily my brother-in-law is the bank manager, so we don't pay any interest.

Nick Well, is there any money still to come in?

Pearl *Calamity Jane* cost seven thousand pounds to put on. We only took three and a half at the box office.

Mona joins them

Mona Thank God neither of you keep a pub. Derek's almost grown a beard waiting for a drink.

Nick You haven't done too badly yourself.

Mona quickly covers her hirsute upper lip with her hand

Pearl Nick and I were discussing finances.

Mona From what I hear there's nothing to discuss.

Pearl gives a dig in the ribs

Nick What do you mean?

Mona Well, there *is* no finance, from what I can gather.

Nick And who's been talking to you? (*He looks at Pearl*) As if I didn't know.

Pearl Well I had to talk to somebody.

She moves away DS *towards Derek*

During Mona and Nick's conversation, Pearl crosses behind them and sits on

*the settee. Derek follows her. She doesn't realize this until she looks up and
sees him*

Mona (*to Nick*) And why shouldn't I know? Why shouldn't everyone
know?

Nick (*taking Mona* DR) Mona, I'd keep this to yourself for the moment if I
were you.

Mona Does the committee know? I bet they don't. I'm sure they'll have
something to say about it.

Nick They'll leave it to me to sort out.

Mona And can you?

Nick I've got out of closer scrapes than this.

Mona Yes, I'll say this for you, you're very good at doing that.

Nick What's that supposed to mean?

Mona Nothing.

Pearl Now look, Derek, if you're going to sit here, I don't want no bloody
nonsense about Deidre.

Derek Oh, that's easy for me. I hardly think about her at all these days.

Nick So what are you suggesting?

Mona I'm suggesting, in view of the money—or lack of it—you do
something small-scale. Well, cheap anyway.

Nick How small-scale?

Mona About twenty people at the most. Something more or less modern-
day, so you don't have a costume bill.

Nick Are you thinking of any show in particular?

Mona *West Side Story* is about the only show that springs to mind.

Nick Mona, that show's been springing to your mind for the last three
years. No. What we need is a backer. A sponsor. Someone who will
plough in a good couple of thou' to put us back on our feet. (*He looks
casually over at Derek. An idea hits him and he begins to smile. He speaks to
Mona but doesn't take his eyes off Derek*)

Mona I still say you'd be better off with my suggestion.

Nick Of course you would.

Mona Do you have any idea how long I've been trying to get my hands on
that show?

Nick Next year, Mona, maybe next year. (*He pauses*) Mona, did you bring
your car?

Mona It's up your drive.

Nick Do me a favour. Would you go and get me some paraffin?

Mona Now?

Nick Yes. If that won't get the barbecue going, nothing will. (*Handing her
his car keys*) There's an empty can in the boot of my car.

Mona (*looking at her watch*) It's a bit late, isn't it?

Nick You'll be all right if you hurry. Take Pearl with you. (*Raising his voice
a little*) You won't mind, will you Pearl?

Derek is deep in conversation with Pearl

Pearl (*eager to break away*) What?

Nick Going with Mona for paraffin.
Pearl No, I don't mind. In fact it will be a pleasure.

Pearl and Mona exit

Nick watches them go. Then he looks over at Derek as he pours himself another drink

Nick (*after a slight pause*) Everything all right, Derek?
Derek Fine ... fine.
Nick Shouldn't be long now.
Derek What?
Nick Then we'll get the old barbecue going.
Derek Oh ... yes.

Nick goes over and sits next to Derek on the settee

Nick Didn't I hear something last week that you're taking on another twenty men at your place?
Derek Yes. It's twenty-five actually.
Nick Expanding, then.
Derek Have to. Need another unit now.
Nick So what's the workforce there?
Derek It'll be just over a hundred with the new lot.
Nick Production must be quite high, then.
Derek We produce more than six million a week.
Nick It makes you wonder where all those balloons go to.
Derek Well, people always have parties, you know. And of course there's Christmas. I'll make a fortune as long as they don't cancel Christmas. And it's not only balloons now—we're moving into condoms as well.
Nick Condoms? I can see you're going to be a very rich man.
Derek Oh, I am already, Nick.

There is a pause

Nick (*standing up*) Can I get you another drink?
Derek No, I'm fine ... fine.

Nick goes to the drinks table

Oh, what's the point of lying? Financially I'm fine, but emotionally I'm in tatters.
Nick Deidre?
Derek Does it show? I thought I've been hiding it pretty well.
Nick I wish there was something I could do to help.
Derek I wish there was, too. I'd do anything to get her back. Anything. (*He pauses*) You're a pretty honest man, Nick. Tell me, what would you do in my position?
Nick (*after a slight pause*) Perhaps if you gave her something. Something she's always wanted and never had.

Derek crosses DL *in front of Nick*

Derek What can you give a woman who has everything?

Nick There must be something. Think.

Derek It's no good—I've lost her, I know. (*He pauses*) Wait a minute . . . there is something. You've never put her in a show, have you?

Nick I've asked her but she's always said no.

Derek I know. But I remember her telling me once, a long time ago, that she always had a secret yearning to play the lead in the show er . . . what was it called now? Shirley Maclaine played it in the film.

Nick *Sweet Charity?*

Derek That's it, *Sweet Charity*. Maybe you can help me out here, Nick.

Nick looks skyward, as if to say "thank you"

Nick How do you mean?

Derek If Deidre was to play that part, maybe she'd be in a better frame of mind, and if she was in a better frame of mind she might be happier, and if she was happier, she might come back to me.

Nick Do you think so?

Derek It's my last shot.

Nick I'd like to help you, Derek—well, both of you. But the thing is . . . the group's in the red. After the news I've had tonight I'm not sure we'll be doing another show.

Derek What sort of red are we talking about?

Nick About ten thousand pounds red.

Derek Oh is that all? No problem.

Nick Pardon?

Derek No problem.

Nick You mean, you're prepared to put up the money?

Derek As long as it's *Sweet Charity* and as long as Deidre gets to play the lead.

Nick I don't want to put you off, but ten thousand pounds is a lot of money.

Derek Peanuts.

Nick Are you sure?

Derek Positive. I can fiddle that on the bloody tax.

Nick (*very pleased with himself*) It's a deal, then.

Derek And just so that there's no backing down on either part—I'm going to write out the cheque now.

He goes and sits at the table. Nick stands just behind him

Nick Have you got a pen?

Derek Yes. (*He takes out his cheque-book and begins to fill it in*) There is one condition.

Nick (*pointing to the top of the cheque*) Nineteenth. August the nineteenth.

Derek Deidre must never know. If she found out that I was at the bottom of it all it will spoil everything. Then the deal's off.

Nick Don't worry—she won't hear a dickie-bird from me.

Derek Just to be on the safe side—I've made it out to September the nineteenth. That will be all right, won't it?

He holds the cheque up to Nick

At this point voices are heard approaching off

Nick recognizes the female voice and grabs the cheque, quickly stuffing it into the breast pocket of his shirt

   Deidre marches on from the right, followed immediately by Eddie

Eddie has a copy of the TV Times *sticking out of his trouser pocket*

Eddie ... yes, you remember. Edna. Edna the inebriated woman.
Nick Deidre!
Derek (*moving quickly away* DL) Oh my God!
Deidre (*stopping dead in her tracks*) Derek!
Eddie (*to Deidre*) Remember her now? Patricia Hayes played it on the telly.

There is a slight pause

Deidre Er ... Nick, this is Edward.
Eddie (*correcting her*) Eddie.
Deidre Eddie. Eddie, this is Nick and Derek. (*She pauses*) Where is everyone?
Nick Some are in the house. Mona and Pearl have gone to get some paraffin. Let me get you both a drink. Deidre?
Deidre (*quickly looking to see what's available*) Er ... punch please.
Nick Freddie?
Eddie (*a little impatiently*) Eddie! It's Eddie, not Freddie.
Nick Sorry. What will you have?
Eddie Is it possible to have a Pimms?
Nick No it's not, actually.
Eddie I'll have a lager, then.
Nick What about you, Derek?
Derek (*without looking at anyone*) Oh, I'm all right, thank you.

Deidre looks at him before going over to him. There is a pause as they look at each other

Deidre I didn't know you were going to be here.
Derek I didn't either. I mean I knew I was going to be here but I didn't know about you. Do you want me to leave?
Deidre Perhaps it's best.
Derek But I don't want to go.
Deidre (*raising her voice*) Well don't then!
Nick (*offering Deidre her drink*) Deidre?
Deidre (*taking it gratefully*) Cheers!

There is an awkward pause

Nick Well ... I think I'll go and tell the others you've arrived.

   Nick runs off into the house

There is a pause

Eddie Does everyone know *Bergerac* starts in about ten minutes?

There is a longer pause

Deidre (*to Derek*) Eddie's mother is in the same ward as my mother.
Derek How is she?
Deidre All right I think. (*To Eddie*) Isn't she?
Derek No, no, I meant *your* mother.
Deidre Oh she's fine . . . she's great. Home one day next week.

There is another pause

Eddie John Nettles. Big fan.
Deidre Eddie's very keen on television. He can tell you everything you don't want to know about it.
Eddie I have one in every room in the house.
Deidre Bit of a fanatic, really.

Roz, Joyce, Teddy and Nick come to the patio door

They keep their distance to see how the land lies

Eddie I've got everything from a twelve to a twenty-six-inch. And look at this—look.

Eddie pushes past Deidre to join Derek on the bench. He holds out his wrist to show Derek, who really isn't interested

Two inches. Gets all the channels. Look. Ever seen Jan Leeming look so small? I'm hoping to get a video for it next year. I'll have to wear that on the other hand, of course.

All of a sudden Derek just cracks up. He gets up and moves behind the bench

Derek (*shouting*) Whhhyyy?? Why did you bring him here?!?
Deidre (*shouting back*) I can bring who I like.
Derek I didn't bring anyone.
Deidre But you could have.
Derek I didn't want to.
Deidre (*screaming*) That's hardly my fault.

The others rush out of the house and make a huge welcoming fuss in order to prevent a row

Teddy rushes out first, wearing a very pretty apron

Teddy (*almost singing it*) Hiya!

Lots of ad-libs from the others

Roz Deidre—you made it.
Deidre I'm sorry I'm late.
Teddy It's all right—you haven't missed anything.
Joyce (*still quite tight*) We haven't even lit the bloody barbecue yet.
Deidre This is Eddie. Eddie, this is Roz, Joyce and Teddy.

All three wave simultaneously, making them look vaguely like "The Three Degrees"

Roz grabs Deidre and takes her over to the settee

Roz (*to Deidre, referring to Derek*) I'm sorry. It wasn't intentional.

Roz and Derek sit on the settee. Joyce joins them

Joyce How's your mother, Deid'?
Deidre Well, she's had her op, did you know?

Joyce nods. The three continue their conversation in mime

Nick (*moving* DL) So what do you do for a living, Eddie?
Eddie I work for "Easylay".
Teddy (*showing immediate interest*) Oooh, hey, is that a brothel?

Nick and Teddy enjoy the little joke. Eddie doesn't have a sense of humour

Eddie It's a battery farm. I grade eggs. (*To Teddy*) What do you do?
Teddy (*winking at Nick*) Well, I'm a barber by trade, but I'm cutting grass in the cemetery at the moment. (*He laughs, then calms down*) No, no, I'm a housing welfare officer actually.
Eddie (*to Nick*) And you?
Nick I run a little newsagent's in the High Street.
Eddie (*still addressing Nick*) Tell me—have you got a big one?

Teddy almost chokes

Nick I beg your pardon?
Eddie Television set.
Teddy Thank God for that!
Nick I don't know. Average I suppose.

At this point Derek, who is at the drinks table drops his glass. Everyone looks round at him. Derek is oblivious to this

Teddy (*to Nick*) I'd better go and give him a hand. (*He goes over to Derek*) Here you are, Derek. Let me help you out, luv.
Derek Oh thank you, Teddy. You're a true friend. (*After a quick mental check*) It is—
Teddy (*jumping in*) Teddy, yes. What are you going to have to drink, kid?
Derek (*pointing to the punch*) I'm on that.
Teddy Are you sure? Perhaps you'd better change to something else. I mean it's pointless now. (*He glances towards Deidre*) You don't want to get too drunk too early, do you?
Derek Teddy—can I tell you something?
Teddy Yes luv, what is it?
Derek I don't want to get drunk.
Teddy Of course you don't.
Derek (*shouting*) I want to get pissed out of my mind!

There is a pause

Teddy Oh, there you are then. (*He pours Derek's punch*) I reckon another
one of these will do it. (*He hands Derek his drink*)

Deidre (*to Roz*) I couldn't get out of it. It had all been arranged before I got
to the hospital.

Roz That's mothers for you.

Deidre If he'd been a decent sort of chap he'd have sensed how embarrassing it all was—played along with it for the sake of our mothers, then gone
our own way when we got outside. I hardly know him, and what I know I
don't like. He hasn't got a car, so it meant I had to bring him here in mine.
He didn't stop talking from the time he got in it. Look at him now.

*They all look over to Nick and Eddie. Eddie is miming away like mad. Nick
covers a yawn*

And it's all rubbish. He's a television freak. I had everything from *Match
of the Day*, to *Songs of Praise*, I felt like crashing the car just to shut him
up.

Eddie (*to Nick*) Oh it's absolutely brilliant. It's written by David Nobbs—
designed by Gloria Clayton and produced by Gareth Gwenlan. You've
got to watch it—it's a must.

Nick But I don't like Leonard Rossiter.

Eddie Don't like Leonard Rossiter? He's brilliant—he's magnificent—he's
incredible.

Nick He's dead.

Eddie Yes I know, they're repeats, I told you that.

Derek What am I going to do, Teddy? (*He grabs Teddy by his shirt-front*)
For God's sake tell me what I'm going to do.

Teddy (*releasing himself from Derek's grip*) Well you can mind that shirt for
a start! (*He pats out the creases*)

Derek I had a suspicion all along that there was someone else. (*He leans on
Teddy's shoulder*) Oh God, I want to die.

Teddy Maybe they're just friends.

Derek Have you seen the way she looks at him?

Teddy No.

Derek She could eat him.

Teddy You mustn't let it get the better of you.

Derek Easy to say—she's not your wife.

Teddy (*taking his drink and moving away* DL) Well she won't be yours after
Monday, luv.

Derek breaks down again, Teddy rushes to him to comfort him

*As Derek is crying on Teddy's shoulder he notices that Eddie leaves Nick and
heads into the house*

Eddie exits into the house

Derek Where's he going now? What's he up to? (*He rushes down to Nick*)
What's happening? Is he leaving? Or has he just gone to use the
bathroom?

Nick He's gone to watch *Bergerac*.

Derek (*to Teddy*) See? See how he treats her? He's gone inside and left her out here.

Teddy There you are then. Got plenty of opportunity now, haven't you?

Derek For what?

Teddy (*pointing with his thumb towards Deidre*) For making your move.

Derek But she doesn't want me to make a move. Well, only home perhaps.

At this moment Mona and Pearl return

Mona One gallon of paraffin.

Pearl is carrying it, but places it down immediately, CS

I'll be giving you a bill, Nick, if I can't get the smell out of my car. Oh hello, Deidre.

Deidre smiles

Roz Right. Let's get to work.

She picks up the can

Nick Perhaps you'd better give that to me.

Roz No indeed. You've failed dismally with that barbecue—now it's time for us women to have a go. Come on, Teddy.

Teddy follows Roz and Joyce into the house

Pearl I need to wash my hands.

Mona I think I do, too.

Pearl You didn't carry it.

Mona I know, but the smell sticks to you.

Pearl Well remember, I was first.

Mona I'll use the bathroom upstairs. That slip of a thing must have finished up there by now.

Pearl and Mona go off into the house

Nick Come to think of it, I haven't seen her for a while. Have you Derek?

Derek What?

Nick Seen Jessica?

Derek I only have eyes for Deidre.

Deidre Oh God, I'm going to be sick.

Nick She hasn't been around for at least half an hour.

Derek Where did you see her last?

Nick Out in the er . . . out here.

Deidre Been decorating, Nick?

Nick No.

Deidre I thought that was paint all down your one side.

Nick (*looking at it*) Oh, it is. Had a little accident out the garage.

Derek (*to Nick, but for Deidre's benefit*) I've been doing a little decorating, a whole lot of decorating. Not me personally. I had it done. Had the whole house done over. Professionally.

There is a pause

Nick I think I'd better check where everyone is.

Deidre and Derek plead with him. Derek wants him to leave so that he can have a word alone with Deidre—she begs Nick not to go as she doesn't want to be left alone with Derek

Deidre No! Don't do that.
Derek Yes—you don't know where she might be.
Deidre She can't be far.
Derek She could be anywhere.
Deidre Don't go, please!
Derek Nick! Nick! (*He pauses*) Just give us five minutes? That's all I want? (*He winks a few times rather obviously at Nick*)

Nick turns to Deidre who very reluctantly gives in and agrees

Deidre All right, five minutes. But I'm warning you, if you start crying, I'll scream.
Derek I won't . . . I promise. No tears—I swear.
Nick Right. I'll leave you then.

Nick goes off to look for Jessica around the front of the house

There is a pause

Derek (*his voice softening*) I suppose you know what Monday is—
Deidre (*jumping in*) Yes.
Derek That chap. What's he got that I haven't?
Deidre Eddie? Nothing! As a matter of fact you're very much alike.

There is a pause before Derek moves closer to her

Derek (*His voice softening*) I suppose you know what Monday is—
Deidre (*jumping in*) Yes.
Derek You haven't had a change of heart—
Deidre (*jumping in again*) No.
Derek Why are you so cruel to me?
Deidre I'm just trying to be civil.
Derek You even brought a man with you.
Deidre I didn't want to bring him here.
Derek He came with you.
Deidre And I didn't know you were going to be here anyway.
Derek (*getting a little worked up*) I still don't think you've been completely honest with me.
Deidre (*a little impatiently*) Derek, I have been honest with you, but you wouldn't recognize the truth if it jumped up and bit you on the nose.
Derek Try me.
Deidre All right, you want the truth? I'll tell you the truth. Regardless of what you think, I didn't leave you for someone else. The truth of the matter is I left you long before I went.

There is a slight pause

Derek I don't understand that.

Deidre Things weren't all right one minute and not the next. Things started falling apart when I told you I'd gone to spend a fortnight with my mother because she was ill, and all the time I was with the girls in Majorca. You didn't ring me, you didn't even ask me how she was. You didn't even twig it when you saw my sun-tan. That's a laugh—you didn't even see my sun-tan. I had to point it out to you.

Derek (*looking very sorry for himself*) Is there something the matter with me?

Deidre Yes there is, and it's time to tell you. You're boring. You're a bore, Derek. A fully-fledged, fully-grown, fully-matured bore!

Derek is hurt. After a moment he turns away and walks towards the bench

Teddy appears in the kitchen window. After looking into the garden and eyeing Derek and Deidre he quickly returns to the kitchen

Derek (*sitting on the bench*) I don't believe you.

Deidre You are—but you don't have to take my word for it.

At this point Nick comes on to the patio, still looking for Jessica

He tries not to disturb them as he goes off in the other direction

Derek Do you think I've always been a bore?

Deidre Oh, yes.

Derek Then why did you marry me?

Deidre (*going to him and sitting next to him on the bench*) Because I was a bore then too.

Derek So what happened?

Deidre I went to night school. Joined the society. I mixed.

Derek I mix.

Deidre Yes, but with other bores. People like yourself. I did something positive about it.

Derek Perhaps I could go to night school. (*He pauses*) Who told you you were a bore?

Deidre I sensed it. If you've got a grain of common sense, after a time you sense it.

Derek (*getting worked up again*) Oh, so you're saying I haven't got any common sense now.

Deidre No, I'm not. You're a very clever man, Derek. You're responsible for the livelihood of an awful lot of people. You're very good at what you do because it's the only thing that you do. It's the only thing you've got time for.

Derek (*looking her straight in the eye*) I could change all that.

Deidre (*looking in his eyes too*) It's too late.

Their heads inch together and they are almost kissing when Deidre breaks away

What am I saying? I don't want you to change anything for me.

Derek You know there's nothing I wouldn't do for you.

Deidre You want to do something for me?

Derek Name it.
Deidre Let me go.

Derek shouts as he gets up and moves away slightly

Derek Why, so that you can marry him?
Deidre (*also standing*) Who?
Derek Eddie or whatever his name is.

Deidre laughs

At this point smoke begins to pour out of the kitchen window. Deidre and Derek remain unaware of it for now

Deidre You really think I'm involved with him?

She moves away DR

I wouldn't jump out of the frying pan into the fire.
Derek Then what's he doing here?
Deidre God knows!
Derek I want to believe you.
Deidre (*exploding*) Derek it doesn't matter to me whether you believe me or
   not! (*She sniffs the air*) Can you smell anything?
Derek It's not me.
Deidre No, burning.

Nick and Jessica enter, appearing from opposite sides of the house

Nick There you are!
Jessica I've been looking for you.
Nick You've been gone ages.
Jessica I've got to talk to you.
Nick Come and have a drink. (*To Derek and Deidre*) That's it, you two . . .
   time's up. (*To Jessica*) Martini?
Derek (*to Deidre*) No. There's something going on between you two.
   There's no smoke without fire.
Jessica (*to Nick*) I've got to go home and change.
Nick Change? No, you look great.
Jessica You don't understand.
Derek (*to Deidre*) Why bring him here? Why tonight?
Deidre I didn't have a choice . . . I was forced into it.

By now smoke is billowing out of the patio doors, too

*Teddy, Roz, Joyce, Mona and Pearl rush out of the house. Teddy carries the
barbecue in his hands. They are all trying to speak at the same time*

Teddy (*heading in Nick's direction*) Gangway . . . gangway . . .

All the women move immediately to the left of the patio

Pearl I can't breathe.
Mona Where's the fire extinguisher?

Teddy, still with the smoking barbecue, rushes over to them

Teddy Take it off me ... take it off me!
Joyce Get him some water ...
Roz Let's get nine-nine-nine.

No one is prepared to relieve Teddy of the burning barbecue. Teddy runs all over the patio like a chicken with its head off

> *Finally he runs off and heads somewhere, maybe towards the front of the house (screaming)*

Teddy Take it off me. (*He screams this several times as he goes*)

Roz, Joyce, Pearl, Deidre and Derek all run out after Teddy, shouting at him as they go

Nick and Jessica turn US *to watch the others as they go. By doing this they should now be standing apart with their backs to the audience, and we see that Jessica has paint marks on her back similar to Nicks. Mona is quick to notice this, and smiles as she turns to face front*

Black-out

ACT II

Scene 1

Later that evening

The barbecue now rests unused against the house wall under the window UL

Roz, Nick, Teddy, Pearl, Joyce, Deidre and Derek are on stage. Derek is sitting on the settee. Nick is far DL keeping an eye on the proceedings. He is also watching the patio doors—he is a little concerned as Mona and Jessica are inside the house together

The women surround Teddy, seated on a chair almost CS. Five or six seconds after the Lights go up they disperse and we see Teddy, who is holding his hands out before him, palms up. Each finger of each hand is individually bandaged

Roz (*moving to Nick*) You could show a little more concern.

Nick I've offered to run him to the hospital.

Roz Ask him how he is.

Nick (*calling across the patio*) How are you, Teddy?

Teddy That's the last bloody barbecue of yours I'll be coming to. Fine lot of friends you all are. (*He means the other women as well*)

The women move to stand behind him

Pearl (*moving a little closer to Teddy*) Oh don't be like that, Teddy.

Roz We did all we could.

Joyce (*moving to Teddy's right*) And Deidre's done a lovely job, fair play. lovely job, fair play.

Pearl (*to Deidre*) Yes, where did you learn first aid?

Derek Night-school.

They all look over their shoulders at Derek

Deidre throws Derek a look, then turns to Teddy

Deidre (*pointing to the bandages*) Let me know if they're a bit tight.

Teddy (*after a slight pause*) It's in me, so I've got to say it. (*Another slight pause. He becomes a little upset. His bottom lip begins to quiver*) Why didn't somebody take it off me?!

Pearl Because you didn't stand still long enough.

Roz I can't understand why you didn't put it down.

Teddy Well, you never think of the right thing to do in a situation like that. (*To the women around him*) Do you?

Joyce Come on now, Ted. Don't bear malice.

Roz It wasn't anyone's fault.

Teddy I suppose you're right—it's just that I felt so bloody silly.
Joyce But you don't feel silly now?

Teddy looks down at his apron and bandaged fingers before looking out front

Teddy Well I do a bit, yes.
Joyce (*trying to make him feel better*) Well, you don't look it.
Teddy Don't I?
Joyce No. Does he, everybody? He doesn't look silly, does he?

There is a chorus of assurance from all the women

Derek is standing, quite drunk by now. He has their attention but doesn't realize it for a few seconds. The women become silent; Derek has the floor

Derek As a matter of fact ... as a matter of fact! (*He sways*) You *do* look stupid, Teddy.

Teddy looks in amazement over at Roz, who is on his left

You're my friend and I won't lie to you. Don't listen to these. If you want the truth—you ask a bore. (*He pauses*) Now I know what you're thinking. You're thinking where are you going to find a bore at this time of night?

Teddy looks over to Deidre

Well, you can ask me. Go on. Ask me how you look.

Teddy looks at all the others before opening his mouth

Teddy How do I look?

Derek draws breath to speak but collapses on the patio before he gets a word out. He is flat on his back. Joyce takes the opportunity to jump on him under the pretence of giving him the kiss of life. But instead of kneeling somewhere near the top half of his body, she is lying on top of him—her lips locked firmly on his. The others, except Deidre on seeing what she's doing, immediately go and drag her off

(*To Deidre*) She's beyond. She is, she's beyond.

The women having got Joyce out of the way, attend Derek, who still seems to be unconscious

Roz Come and give us a hand, Nick.

Nick crosses and helps carry Derek

Nick We'd better put him on the settee, I think.

Nick, Roz and Pearl do this

Teddy I'd give you a hand but I haven't got a good one. (*He laughs as he holds up his hands*)
Roz (*returning to Teddy's left*) I feel it's all my fault, you know.
Teddy Don't be silly. I don't blame you personally.
Roz (*looking at Derek, who is now outstretched on the settee*) He's going to have a hell of a head in the morning.

Teddy (*realizing she meant Derek and not him*) Oh . . .

Roz (*as an afterthought*) And how are you, Teddy?

Teddy (*holding up his hands*) They're throbbing like hell.

Deidre Yes, they will for a couple of days.

Teddy (*to Roz*) How am I going to manage?

Roz What do you mean?

Teddy Well I know I think I'm a bit of a clever bugger, but there's a limit to what I can do with two thumbs. (*He wiggles them and winces with pain*)

Roz Of course, I hadn't thought of that. You're never going to cope in that state on your own.

Teddy I'm not, am I?

Deidre Can't you have home help?

Teddy (*outraged*) Home help? How old do you think I am?

Deidre I didn't know age came into it. I thought you only had to be disabled to qualify.

Teddy (*shouting*) I'm not bloody disabled either, luv. (*To Roz*) You listen to her, see, and I'm just about ready for sheltered accommodation.

Deidre I didn't mean . . .

Teddy (*at the end of his tether*) Now look, Deidre . . . I'm not being funny, right? I'm not being funny but my nerves are rrrraw! So if I were you, I'd either shut my gob, or go over there (*he points towards the settee*) and give a hand with your husband.

Deidre He's not my husband!

Teddy It's not Monday yet, luv . . .

Roz Have a drink, Teddy. Perhaps that will calm you down.

She moves to the drinks table

Teddy Yes, go on, all right. Look, I'm a bath of sweat!

Roz (*at the table*) What are you going to have?

Teddy I'll have a morphine with ice and lemon.

Roz makes him a gin

Deidre (*to Teddy*) Is it very painful?

Teddy PAINFUL? I feel like a gynaecologist on overtime.

Joyce kneels in front of the settee, still fussing over Derek

Joyce Nick, come and have a look at Derek—he hasn't come round yet. And bring a brandy with you.

Nick immediately pours one

Teddy (*to Pearl*) I said he looked a funny colour earlier on.

Deidre There's nothing wrong with him. I've seen him like that before.

Teddy Well he doesn't look right to me. What do you say, Pearl?

Nick takes the drink over to Joyce, who drinks it herself. Teddy, Roz, Deidre and Pearl are gobsmacked. Nick goes round the back of the settee and examines Derek from there

Nick It wouldn't be a bad idea if someone took him home.

Deidre (*slight pause*) Don't look at me.

Teddy And I don't drive, Nick, as well you know.

Nick (*getting himself a drink*) Looks as though he'll have to kip here, then.

Teddy Well, don't give him my room.

Nick Your room?

Teddy (*holding up his hands yet again*) Hey luv, I'm not going anywhere in this state!

Joyce Deidre, I think you'd better come over here and have a look at Derek.

Deidre Why me?

Teddy You're his wife.

Joyce You're half a nurse or something, aren't you?

Nick He's only drunk.

Joyce No, Nick. I think it might be a bit more serious than that.

Deidre How do you mean?

Joyce Well, I've been drunk in my time—

Teddy You can say that again.

Joyce But I still breathed.

There is a pause. Everyone except Teddy and Roz rushes over to the settee to examine Derek. Deidre feels for a pulse

Roz (*to Teddy*) We should never have given him that punch.

Teddy (*full of remorse*) I know.

Nick, Pearl and Joyce move away, leaving Deidre still checking for some sort of life. Another pause

Roz Everything all right, Deid'?

Deidre (*still looking for a pulse*) I can't get a pulse.

There is complete silence. Deidre lets go of his hand and it flops almost to the ground. Deidre steps back before turning to the others to announce

I'm afraid he's dead.

There is another pause as everyone is struck dumb by Deidre's announcement

After a moment, Derek farts—although he is still unconscious

Teddy (*shocked but about to burst out laughing*) Well I've heard of the last breath but that's ridiculous.

Deidre Someone else had better try. Who else knows how to look for a pulse?

Teddy I do—but I'm not going to feel much through these, am I? (*Indicating his bandages*)

Deidre Joyce? Pearl, what about you?

Pearl I'm not sure what a pulse feels like.

Teddy Pull the other one.

Pearl I'm not—really.

Teddy It's like a throb only smaller. Know now, don't you?

Pearl (*to Roz*) You try—I'm not very good at doing that.

Roz What makes you think I am?

Nick is already looking for a pulse, and has just found one

Nick It's all right. Panic over.

Teddy That's a laugh ... who panicked?

Nick He's okay. Had us worried there for a minute, Deidre.

Deidre Well. I don't understand it. He didn't have a pulse a minute ago.

Teddy Ohh, don't sound so disappointed.

Deidre crosses over towards the bench to sit down

Joyce (*walking over to join Deidre*) Hey, Deid' ... imagine if he had, you know ...

Deidre What?

Joyce Died. You'd have been a very merry widow.

Teddy (*calling over to them*) Now don't go putting ideas into her head.

Joyce (*to Deidre*) Imagine if he'd snuffed it after Monday. You wouldn't have had a penny.

Deidre Money's never bothered me.

Teddy and Roz look at each other

Nick May as well let him sleep it off here. Roz, nip in the house and get something to slip over him, will you?

Roz starts to go into the house

Mona appears through the patio doors, and walks down onto the patio

Mona Attention everyone. Attention. A little surprise. Jessica has put on something and I'd like you to tell me what you think of it ... (*Calling to Jessica*) Come out. Come out. Come on, don't be shy.

Jessica comes out on to the patio wearing a red Puerto-Rican style dress. She looks like Maria in West Side Story

Well now ... what do you think about that?

No one replies

Isn't she just perfect for Maria?

Teddy I've never seen anyone look less like a nun.

Mona I'm talking about *West Side Story*, not *The Sound of Music*. I can get all the costumes for the entire show. I have a connection with the Baron Heath players. They did it two years ago. What do you think, Nick?

Teddy (*to Mona*) You don't give up, do you? (*To the others*) We have this with her year in year out.

Mona I just think it's a marvellous choice under the circumstances.

Teddy What circumstances?

Mona It's cheap and we're broke.

Teddy Is that right, Nick?

Nick I don't know what the cost of the show is.

Teddy I mean are we broke?

Nick I can still put my hands on a couple of quid.

Teddy Oh well, that's all right then.

Mona (*stiffening*) So you won't consider it, then?

Nick I'm afraid not.

Mona (*staring at him*) Right! You're going to be sorry for this, you wait and see.

Nick looks a little uneasy. Mona sits down in a huff. There is a long pause

Teddy Happy days. (*Another pause*) Hey, did anyone see *South Pacific* last week?

Pearl No, I missed it.

Teddy I wish I had.

Pearl What was it like?

Teddy Bloody awful. Wasn't it, Nick?

Nick Scenery was nice.

Teddy Emile was like that. (*He holds up his index finger*) And without the bandage. You should have seen him ... he was like the road. He looked full of T.B. to me. He kept turning upstage every two minutes. I thought he had the giggles but apparently he had a pump!

Deidre I heard excellent reports.

Teddy Did you hear about Nellie? She had the right name. She was sixteen stone if she was an ounce. She had hair in a pony-tail way down her back, which wasn't difficult as she was only four foot three. They were a pair well-matched but they looked like something from the *Rocky Horror Show*.

Deidre Apparently they sang well.

Teddy Not the night I was there.

Deidre Anyone can have an off night.

Teddy Off night? They were so bad I went twice!

Pearl Oh Teddy ... you're awful unkind.

Teddy Hey luv, that's nothing to what they say about us.

Mona Yes, we were the laughing stock last year. (*She throws a look at Joyce*)

Joyce nods and laughs in agreement, then realizes the dig was at her. She cries as she sits in a chair at the drinks table

Pearl and Roz go to Joyce to comfort her. Teddy joins in but remains seated in his chair

Teddy (*to Joyce*) Take no notice of her luv ... she's a cow. Nothing but an old cow!

Jessica (*raising her voice above the others*) Have you heard yourselves? Have you heard what you sound like? Anyone would think you're all God's gift.

Teddy Ohhh, hark at the Queen of the Pantomime.

Jessica It's about time someone told you a couple of home truths.

Teddy She hasn't been with the company two minutes and already she wants to speak her mind. Listen luv, let me tell you something. Nobody says what they think in this society. Not unless they're either leaving it, playing the lead, or pissed! Isn't that right, Nick?

Nick smiles and nods

Jessica I just don't think you're in a position to criticize.

Teddy I'm entitled to an opinion the same as anyone else. Anyway, a bit of criticism never hurt anyone.

Jessica It hurt Joyce.

Joyce (*still upset, she stands up*) What happened to me could happen to anyone.

Deidre She forgot a line, that's all.

Teddy It's happened to us all over the years.

Jessica I'm not talking about the line she forgot. I'm talking about the seven and a half minutes she ad-libbed on her own.

Joyce cries even more

Teddy She had what's known in the business as a black-out.

Jessica She had what's known in the business as a brain-storm—brought on by the half a bottle of vodka she drank before curtain up.

Joyce That's not true. Nick doesn't allow drinking backstage. Do you, Nick?

Nick That's right, Joyce.

Jessica I know that and you know it. That's why you kept it in a lemonade bottle.

Joyce I don't have to stand for this.

Teddy Of course you don't ... sit down, luv, and ignore her.

Jessica Some people might put your performance down to the nervous break-down which immediately followed it—but we all know the real reason. Don't we Joyce, luv?

Teddy Ohhh, the bitch!

Jessica crosses in front of the drinks table and goes far DR in front of the settee. On her way, though, she turns on her very high heel, but carries on regardless. As she passes Teddy she blows a bubble at him with her gum

Roz This is all getting far too personal.

Pearl Quite right.

Teddy (*to Roz*) When you asked us to come to this barbecue, I didn't think for one minute it was us who were going to be roasted!

Roz Let's all have another drink and forget about it. (*She goes to the table*)

Teddy Good idea. (*To Joyce*) All right now luv?

Joyce fights back a tear and nods

Nick wanders DR to Jessica

Nick Was there any need for that?

Jessica I don't know who they think they are.

Teddy (*to Joyce*) I don't know who she thinks she is.

Nick You don't half pick your moments.

Jessica Well if they didn't know what to make of me before, they do now.

Nick (*indicating the dress*) I quite like you in that.

Jessica Careful.

Nick Red's your colour.

Jessica It's my temperament too. (*Slight pause*) I don't know what to do about my dress.

Nick Get rid of it—I'll buy you a new one.

Jessica I can't. She won't give it back to me.

Nick Mona?

Jessica nods

Jessica She says she wants to hang on to it. Says she has some stuff at home that will get the paint off no problem.

Nick (*suspiciously*) Did she? She's up to something. (*Calling to her*) Mona? (*He beckons her over*)

Mona crosses and goes over to Nick and Jessica

Deidre (*to Joyce*) I shouldn't take any notice of her if I were you.

Roz You're too sensitive by half, that's your trouble.

Taking Joyce's arm, she nods to the others that she's taking her down to sit on the bench . . . far away from the drinks table. Joyce is still unsteady on her feet, and Pearl and Deidre help move her

Joyce (*drunk and upset again*) Seven and a half minutes! (*Shouting*) Seven and a half minutes, she said! Cheeky little bugger. She must have had a stop watch.

They are all sitting down on the bench now

Deidre (*trying to make Joyce feel better*) Well, I know I'm only the prompt— and you did almost give me a heart attack, I must say that—but I thought it was quite an accomplishment.

Joyce (*very glad to hear it*) Did you?

Deidre (*reassuringly*) Yes.

Roz It was. I keep telling her that. (*Quite proud*) I can't think of anyone who could leave the script for so long, sing two songs from a different show, then pick up where they left off.

Joyce begins to pull herself together a little

Pearl I've got to be honest with you, Joyce—I wouldn't have known anything was wrong. If you hadn't gone into that ventriloquist act, I wouldn't have suspected anything.

Nick (*to Mona*) She'd like it back.

Mona You would, you mean.

Nick What good is it to you?

Mona Oh, you'd be surprised.

Nick It doesn't belong to you.

Mona Neither does she.

Nick Who?

Mona Jessica—belong to you.

They stare at each other—Mona wearing a broad knowing smile

Nick I want the dress back.

Mona I'll make a deal with you. If you do *West Side Story* I'll give it to you. If you don't—I'll give it to Roz.

Roz (*calling to Nick and Mona*) Come on, you two. Let's try something on the barbecue. (*She is about to move in its direction*)

Teddy (*to Roz*) No, no, no. You can't cook anything yet. You've got to wait for the coals to glow.

Pearl How long will that take?

Teddy About half an hour.

Pearl Half the night's gone.

Teddy I got an idea. What about announcing the show now? I mean, I think we've waited long enough.

Jessica (*excitedly, to Nick*) Yes! Announce the show now, Nick.

Teddy I don't know what you're sounding so excited for.

Jessica I might have got every reason to.

Teddy Oh? Do you know something I don't?

Joyce (*shouting over to him*) Don't bite, Teddy.

Teddy You're right, I shouldn't, I know.

Nick (*firmly*) How many times have I got to tell you, no-one knows what the show is. At the moment I'm not sure of it myself.

Teddy And what's that supposed to mean?

Nick I'm going to need ten minutes. I've got to make a couple of phone calls.

Nick exits into the house

Joyce I don't think I can stand the suspense much longer.

Teddy Don't worry, Joyce luv. I think we're home and dry. (*He winks at her and laughs*)

Jessica mocks his laugh as she moves away DR

Teddy goes and joins Joyce on the bench

Oohhh, I don't know what I'll do if I'm cast opposite her!

Joyce You'll be the true professional you are, Teddy, and not let it make any difference.

Teddy I suppose you're right.

Deidre I wish I had the guts to go on stage.

Pearl You need a bit more than guts, luv.

Deidre What's that show we all saw a couple of years ago? Christine Bradshaw was in it. She sang that song, "If They Could See Me Now".

Joyce *Sweet Charity.*

Teddy *Charity*, yes.

Deidre That's right. I thought she was marvellous.

Joyce I've played that.

Teddy I know luv, you were fabulous. Fabulous!

Deidre Not that I ever could, or would, but that's the part for me.

Pearl I suppose we all see ourselves differently to what we are. I mean, I'm still waiting to be asked to play Gypsy.

Deidre You're too old.

Pearl Rose then. Her mother.

Joyce That's more like it. Marvellous part, done it twice.

Teddy (*to the others*) Saw her both times. Fabulous, fabulous!

Deidre You're like me though, Pearl. You'd die wouldn't you, if you had to go on stage?

Pearl Oh yes. I'm all chops, but I could never pretend to be someone else.

Mona (*now sitting at the drinks table*) Some people take to it like a duck to water.

Joyce It's like everything else, Mona. The younger you start the better you are at it.

Mona You must have been drinking at the age of three then.

Joyce (*trying to stand*) What's this, pick on Joyce night, is it?

Teddy sits her back down

Roz Come on now, Mona. We're all going to make the effort to be nice to each other.

Pearl Shouldn't that include Jessica as well?

Roz Yes. (*She stands behind Teddy*) You call her over, Teddy?

Teddy Why me?

Roz 'Cause you're the man.

Mona Huh!

Teddy throws Mona a rotten look

Teddy (*after eyeing Jessica for a second, calling over to her*) Oi, smart arse!

Roz Teddy!

Teddy (*overdoing the friendly bit*) Want to come an sit over by us, luv?

Jessica No!

Teddy (*immediately*) Oh, please your bloody self, then.

Pearl Oh come on Jessica—it is a bit of a party after all.

Teddy Party? It's more like a religious holiday. I feel as if I've given up eating for Lent.

Mona (*impatiently*) Didn't you have something before you came?

Roz (*jumping in*) Remember, Teddy, we're being nice.

Teddy (*sickly nice*) I didn't actually, Mon'. Did you?

Mona I had a roll about four o'clock.

Teddy Hey luv, I had a roll about—

Roz (*shouting*) Teddy!

Pearl (*to Teddy*) Almost forgot yourself.

Teddy (*laughing*) I get carried away.

Mona I wish you would!

Teddy (*immediately changing from laughter to extreme anger*) See? Now it's not only me!

Roz Calm down, Teddy, for God's sake.

Deidre They're like cat and dog. I don't know why you invite them.

Roz I'm beginning to wonder myself.

Pearl I think we ought to have a box. Like a swear box—only a bitch box. And every time someone makes a bitchy remark, they'll have to put some money in it. All the funds can go to the society—God knows, they need it.

Deidre That's a good idea.

Teddy You bugger off. I'm not doing that. I'll have to put my pay in it. (*Nodding towards Mona*) And with the proceeds from me and her we'll be able to do *Gone With The Wind* next year.

At this point Eddie enters from the house, carrying the television set

Roz (*to Eddie*) What's going on?

Eddie Terrible reception in there. Thought I'd try it out here—see if it's any better.

Teddy (*to Roz*) No! Don't have him out here. (*To Eddie*) Apparently the reception is marvellous up in the attic.

Eddie Where's your aerial?

Roz It's on the extension. There it is, look—you can just see it.

Eddie I'm sure I can improve it for you. Mind if I try?

Roz Yes!

Teddy No! (*To Eddie*) You carry on. (*To Roz*) Let him get on with it. Anything as long as he's out of our hair. (*To Pearl and Deidre*) Don't you agree?

Eddie goes back indoors with the television

Roz (*to Teddy*) What'll Nick say?

Teddy Oh bugger Nick.

Mona gives Teddy a look

Why are you looking at me like that?

She looks away

(*To everyone else*) Why did she look at me like that then?

Deidre She didn't look like anything.

Teddy Yes, she did.

Pearl You're getting paranoid, Teddy.

Teddy I'm getting hungry.

Roz What if I make you a salad roll?

Teddy Anything. My stomach thinks my throat's been cut.

Roz Anyone else while I'm at it?

Generally, no, they'll all wait. She goes to a small table which is right of the patio doors to make the roll

Mona (*referring to Jessica*) It makes you wonder why she doesn't have a young man, doesn't it?

Teddy No, it doesn't surprise me.

Pearl, Deidre and Joyce are in full agreement

She's an old cow. (*To Joyce*) Isn't she?

Joyce I can think of a better word than that.

General hubble bubble as they discuss it

Jessica is watching them from across the other side of the patio. She shouts over to them

Jessica (*shouting*) Oi!

They all stop talking and look over to her

Are you lot talking about me, there?

A slight pause. All the women and Teddy look at each other before looking back over at Jessica

Mona
Pearl } (*as if butter wouldn't melt in their mouths*) No.
Joyce
Teddy

Jessica That's all right, then.

Mona I was only saying that you don't seem to have a young man.

Jessica I've got a fella.

Mona Really.

Pearl You've never brought him to rehearsals.

Mona (*wickedly*) Perhaps he's already there.

Roz (*still at the table*) What do you mean?

Mona Well, maybe she has someone and keeps him rather quiet.

Roz Is that right, Jessica?

Jessica That's right, yeah.

Roz So you're a little dark horse?

Teddy Aye, and be careful, cause I'm sure that bugger kicks.

Roz brings Teddy's roll to him. She sits on the arm of the bench and holds the roll to Teddy's mouth so he may bite into it, as he can't hold it for himself

Deidre Is it anyone we know?

Jessica I can't tell you that.

Pearl Why not?

Jessica Because he's a married man.

Teddy Well, all you can deduce from that, folks, is that it's not me.

Eddie enters from inside the house and immediately exits R

No one pays him any attention

Joyce I had an affair once.

Teddy Aye—with the Treorchy Male Voice Choir.

Deidre What happened?

Joyce I told his wife.

Pearl Did you?

Deidre What did you do that for?

Joyce Long story.

Pearl What did she say?

Joyce She said she already knew.

Pearl Did she leave him?

Joyce Eventually.

Deidre Tell us what happened.

Joyce He couldn't cope with it and turned to drink. We would have got engaged, but neither of us could stay sober long enough.

Pearl What happened to him?

Joyce We split and went our separate ways. I went off to Cardiff to play Dolly for Orbit—

Teddy (*to the others*) Should have seen her. She was fabulous. Fabulous!

Joyce And the last I heard, he'd had a liver transplant.

Teddy And if you're not careful, you'll be having a bugger next.

Joyce What do you mean? This is only lemonade.

Teddy Pull the other one.

Joyce (*insisting*) It *is*.

Teddy If that's lemonade, my name's John Hanson.

Joyce Roz?

Roz That's right. Lemonade with a dash of Martini.

Teddy (*to Joyce*) Let me taste it.

Joyce No.

Teddy Come on, give Ted a taste.

Joyce (*reluctantly*) All right. (*She holds the glass for him*) But watch the divers. (*She's referring to the crumbs in his mouth from the roll*)

Teddy (*after tasting it, bursting into song*) "My desert is waiting ..." (*He laughs*)

The others join in the laughter

That's more like Martini with a dash of lemonade.

Joyce Bugger off. I think you must have burnt your taste-buds as well as your bloody fingers, luv.

They all laugh at this

Derek throws off the blanket and tries to pull himself up to a sitting position on the settee. Teddy sees him doing this

Teddy (*to all the girls*) Oh God, look. (*Nodding over towards Derek*) Curse of the living dead.

Derek Where's Deidre? Whose house am I in? (*He sees Jessica, who is just to his right. He gets up and goes to her*) Excuse me. Do I know you?

Jessica No.

Derek Who am I? (*Correcting himself quickly*) I mean who are you?

Jessica Jessica.

Derek I'm Derek.

Teddy (*to the women*) This should be fun.

Derek Do you know me?

Jessica I know who you are.

Derek Who am I, then?

Jessica You're Derek.

Derek (*pleased*) That's right. I wonder if I can have a word? Will you come
and sit down?

They move to sit on the settee

Teddy Oh, that's it Deidre—you've lost him. I think they've clicked.
Deidre (*going to the drinks table*) I should be so lucky.
Derek Tell me Jessica—have you known me long?
Jessica Not really, no.
Derek How do I strike you?
Jessica Pardon?
Derek What do you make of me?
Jessica You don't really want me to tell you.
Derek Oh but I do. I must know. You won't hurt my feelings.
Jessica I hardly know you.
Derek All the better—no holds barred—the truth is very important to me
tonight. Come on, tell me. What was your first impression of me?
Jessica (*after a slight pause*) What a fart!
Derek (*after a slight pause*) Right I see. And your second impression?
Jessica God, what a boring fart!
Derek (*after a slight pause*) Thank you. Thank you Jessica. You're a true
friend.
Jessica I'm not your friend at all, luv.
Derek No, perhaps not. But you're a true something, whatever.

Mona comes to join them, followed by Deidre

Mona Better after your little sleep, Derek?
Derek Did I drop off? I didn't mean to. I seem to do that a lot lately.

Deidre takes Jessica and leads her to the other side of the patio

Mona You're not sleeping properly in the night, that's your trouble.
Derek Hardly surprising under the circumstances.
Deidre (*to Jessica*) Excuse me. I hope you don't find this too embarrassing,
but I must ask you. This man you're involved with—this married man.
(*Slight pause*) It's not Derek, is it?
Jessica (*screaming as she laughs*) Derek?

She moves away, laughing as she goes

   Eddie enters from the R

He drags a set of double ladders on to the patio

Derek Mona, you seem to be a very straight sort of person to me.
Mona Oh I am, Derek.
Derek If you had to describe me in a couple of words—what would you
say?
Mona Couple of words?

   Derek, I could sum you up in one.
Derek Yes?

Mona Boring.

A slight pause

Derek Thank you very much indeed.
Mona Don't mention it.

Joyce joins them, carrying two drinks

Joyce Dare you have another drink, Derek?
Mona (*to Joyce*) Dare you?
Joyce Oh, shut up!
Derek Ta. Joyce?
Joyce That's my name.
Derek Joyce, am I a nice person?
Joyce I suppose so.
Derek Then why doesn't anyone like me?
Joyce (*affectionately*) Cause you're boring, luv.

Eddie goes over to the others on the bench

Eddie Sorry.

They all look at him

Roz What?
Eddie Sorry. I'm sorry.
Teddy For what?
Eddie For interrupting. I need a hand.
Teddy (*holding his up*) Sorry luv, you're out of luck.
Roz What do you want a hand for?
Eddie I got to get at the aerial.
Roz There isn't any need, you know.
Eddie No, I want to. It's a challenge and I want to put it right for you. It's not going to take two minutes.
Roz But there's nothing wrong with the television.
Eddie Nothing wrong? (*He laughs, before addressing the others*) Nothing wrong with it, she says. (*To Roz*) It's full of snow. Only needs a small adjustment to the aerial. Perhaps if you ladies would just hold the bottom.
Teddy (*to Roz*) Go on—sort him out. Perhaps he'll leave us in peace then.

Deidre and Pearl sigh but agree to help. They go over to where the ladder is

  Roz goes indoors

Teddy Hey, want to help two damsels in distress?
Joyce We *are* two damsels in distress.
Teddy Well, I've come to rescue you.
Mona Some knight in armour.
Teddy Go and help Deidre and Pearl.

Mona and Joyce stand

  (*To Joyce, whispering*) I'll hold the fort here. But if I don't get away in five minutes . . . come and get me.

Mona and Joyce join Deidre and Pearl, helping to erect the ladder

Derek (*standing, referring to Joyce and Mona*) Lovely people. You're all nice really. Truthful. Honest. I like that in a person. I can see why Deidre thinks so much of you all.

Teddy Friends are not everything, Derek.

Derek They mean an awful lot to me tonight.

Teddy (*pausing slightly*) Oh, there you are then.

Derek I've been thinking. I need to do something. (*He pauses*) Apparently, Teddy, apparently, I'm boring. Now if this is true, and there's strong feeling that it is—I've decided to do something about it.

Teddy Good for you.

Derek But I'm not sure what. (*Pausing*) I wish I was a bit like you.

Teddy (*smiling, he feels flattered*) Do you?

Derek Yes ... well you're so ... how can I put it? So cock sure of yourself.

Teddy (*coyly*) Oh I don't know about that.

Derek How do I go about being a little more like you?

Teddy (*Pausing*) Well there's this club in Cardiff I spend a lot of time in. If you like, next time I go I'll take you with me.

Derek Club? Yes I think I'd like that. And will it help me to come out more?

Teddy Derek, if it's in you ... it'll bring it out, kid.

Eddie ascends the ladder. Mona, Joyce and Pearl are holding it

Derek Tell me, Teddy. What's the first lesson in being able to mix?

Teddy Well, I always start off with a good joke.

Derek (*disappointed*) Oh ... I don't know any.

Teddy Come off it. You've got a factory full of men. You must have heard a yarn or two.

Derek I do hear some occasionally—but I never understand them.

Teddy That doesn't matter, as long as you pretend to.

Derek And how do I do that?

Teddy You laugh at the end of it!

Derek nods but Teddy isn't convinced that he fully understands

Listen to this. There were these two rhinoceroses, right? Betty and Binny. They both got dolled up and went to a disco. When they got there, Binny fancied this other rhino, who was already up on the floor, dancing. All night she waited for him to come over and ask her to dance but he never did. In the end she said to Betty, "I've had a guts full of this," she said. "If he's not going to ask me to dance, I'm going over to ask him." Betty said, "You're not," Binny said, "I am—watch me". So over she went and tapped in. Anyway, there they were now dancing, and he said, "I've been watching you". "Oh aye?" she said. "Yes," he said. "What's your name?" and she said "Binny, what's yours?" And he said, "Neil". And with that she collapsed in a heap on the floor. Everybody rushed round—Betty got there first. She tapped Binny on the face a couple of times and sure enough, slowly Binny came round. "What's the matter with you?" Betty said. "Oh I couldn't help it", she said. "I couldn't help it, but I've never danced with Rhino Neil [Ryan O'Neal] before".

Teddy laughs helplessly. Derek hasn't understood it. After a time Teddy realizes this

Oh Derek, I give up with you.

Derek What should I have done?

Teddy (*exploding*) Laughed, for God's sake!

Derek Try me again. Just say the last bit so's I can have a go.

Teddy (*pausing slightly before taking a deep breath and saying it in one go*) Binny collapsed on the floor—Betty tapped her on the cheek—she came round—she said what's the matter—she said I couldn't help it, but I've never danced with Rhino Neil before!

Derek forces a hysterical laugh

Teddy All right, Derek ... don't overdo it.

Roz appears at the patio doors

Roz (*calling*) Derek?

He turns to look at her

Nick wants a word.

Derek With me?

Deidre notices this

Roz Yes.

Teddy (*to Roz*) What's he doing in there?

Roz He's still on the telephone. He's speaking to our Chairman.

Teddy Chairman?

Roz and Derek go inside

Jessica (*to Deidre*) What's going on?

Deidre shakes her head

Is something happening?

Deidre Nick's speaking to the Chairman, that's all.

Jessica So there's nothing to worry about?

Deidre Like what?

Jessica I don't know. Last minute change of plan or something.

Deidre I wouldn't have thought so.

Jessica Oh that's all right then—because I've got my heart set on *Gigi*. I'd scratch his eyes out if I didn't get to play it now.

Deidre Whose eyes?

Jessica Nick's.

Deidre Are you telling me the next show is *Gigi*?

Jessica Yeah.

Deidre But Nick doesn't tell anyone.

Jessica He told *me*.

The action shifts to Mona and Pearl

Pearl (*to Mona*) What makes you think that?

Mona He's a man, isn't he? All men are weak.

Pearl (*moving* DS *a little from the ladder*) I don't see that as a reason for changing the show. If he's not going to change it for financial reasons, he's not going to change it for you.

Mona (*joining her*) You mustn't underestimate my powers of persuasion.

Eddie (*from the top of the ladder*) Oi!

Mona and Pearl rush back to grip the ladder

Pearl So what do you reckon it's going to be then?

Mona I'm finally going to have my way and show my talent as dance mistress.

Pearl You don't mean *West Side Story*?

Mona nods

He can't cast it.

Mona Oh, I don't know. I'm looking at a very good Maria.

Pearl follows Mona's gaze to find she is looking at Jessica and Deidre

Joyce and Teddy take up the conversation, moving to sit on the settee as they do so

Joyce Must be something in the wind. Nick wouldn't ring the Chairman for nothing!

Teddy It's obvious what it is. He's changed the show, hasn't he?

Joyce What was the show then?

Teddy Oh I don't know what it was, but it's *Oklahoma* now. Oohhh, I'm going to play Curly at last.

Joyce (*standing up and moving forward a step or two*) Oh, what a comeback for me. And to be playing opposite you.

Teddy stands and joins her. He is grinning like a Cheshire cat

We haven't done that since *New Moon*. Remember, Ted?

Teddy Nineteen seventy-three.

Joyce positions herself next to Teddy in the pose they adopted for the duet

Joyce Act two.

They both begin to sing "Wanting You"

Joyce sings the low note and Teddy takes the high note

After they have finished the company applaud. Teddy and Joyce remain in their pose for a beat or two

Teddy Hey, listen Joyce, luv. I've got a bit of a problem.

Joyce Tell me, Ted. You know you can tell me anything after that.

Slight pause

Teddy I want a pee.

Joyce looks at him. Teddy moves his arm and shows her his bandaged fingers

Joyce Oh, hell.

Teddy Awkward, innit?

Joyce Can't you wait till Nick comes off the telephone?

Teddy (*holding himself a certain way*) No. I'm having trouble with my water works and I can't hold it in long.

Joyce I don't know what to suggest. (*She turns to the others*) Anybody got any ideas? Teddy needs to use the bathroom.

Mona (*as if insulted*) What can we do?

Teddy Well it's a bit bloody difficult for me at the minute, isn't it? I need a hand.

Pearl You'll have to wait and ask one of the men.

Teddy I can't.

Mona What do you expect us to do? I'm not touching it.

Teddy I only want a pee. You won't have to come in with me. I just need someone to undo the top of my trousers and my zip.

Pearl You're still not going to manage.

Teddy Yes I will.

Joyce (*to Teddy*) Who's going to get it out for you?

Teddy They won't have to. I won't stand up. I'll crouch down to do it. (*He indicates the action slightly as he says it*)

Mona (*to Pearl*) I assumed that's what he did anyway.

Teddy Bitch! Well, any volunteers? Come on, form a queue.

Joyce What about you, Deidre? You're half a nurse or something, aren't you?

Deidre I've done a little first-aid, that's all.

Joyce Well what do you think? Can you help Teddy out?

Deidre (*sighing*) Well if no one else will, I suppose I'll have to, won't I?

She goes to Teddy

Teddy The top button.

She puts her hand under his apron and attempts to undo it. She has difficulty

Deidre Breath in.

Teddy I *am* breathing in.

Deidre (*still struggling*) Perhaps you should lose some weight.

Teddy Perhaps you should shut your bloody gob!

Deidre releases him and is about to return to her seat

Deidre Fair enough then.

Teddy (*desperately*) No, Deidre! I'm sorry ... I didn't mean it. Come back, come on.

There is a slight pause

I'm desperate, gul.

Deidre obliges and eventually succeeds in undoing the button

Teddy (*with some relief*) There you go. Now the zip.

She has even more trouble with the zip. After several attempts she goes on to her knees. She can't see what she's trying to do, so innocently she lifts up the apron

Deidre (*holding up the apron*) Hang on to that, Teddy.

Deidre's head is very close to Teddy's crotch. Teddy, holding the apron with his two available thumbs, equally innocently begins to let the apron down over Deidre's head. As she undoes the zip, Teddy sighs with relief

> *At this moment Derek comes out of the house to stand just outside the patio doors*

Derek (*rushing to Deidre*) Deidre, don't do it. For God's sake, don't do it!
Deidre (*appearing from under the apron*) Don't do what? I'm only doing him a favour.
Derek Yes, I can see that.
Teddy (*holding his hands to his waist in order to keep his trousers up*) She was only helping me out, Derek. Couldn't do it myself see, could I?
Derek (*firmly*) I want to know what's going on?
Teddy (*rushing past him on his way into the house*) I'd be happy to explain, Derek, but I've got to rush.

Teddy exits into the house

On the way he bumps into Nick, who is just entering

Derek (*after a slight pause*) Well ... I'm waiting.
Joyce It's all right, Derek. Deidre was helping Teddy to open his trousers. There was nothing in it.
Deidre (*to Derek*) You didn't honestly think I was doing anything with Teddy? Not that it has anything to do with you if I was.
Eddie (*climbing down the ladder, holding the aerial*) Now listen. This aerial's no good where it is. It's got to go on to the main roof of the house.
Nick Are you sure?
Eddie Positive. I'm the expert! Now I'll put it on this table for safe keeping. Now no bugger touch it please, there's good people. (*He places the aerial on the small table—R of the patio doors*)

Eddie exits into the house

Nick (*clapping his hands*) Right. Everyone okay for drinks? (*Looking around*) You're not, I can see. (*He goes to the drinks table*) Come on—come and get your refills.

Joyce, Mona, Pearl and Jessica join Nick at the table

Derek and Deidre are left alone for a moment

Derek I'm sorry if I got the wrong end of the stick.
Deidre Derek, you got the wrong stick!
Derek I still feel very protective of you.

Deidre Well, don't.

Derek I can't help myself. (*Pausing*) Well, that's not absolutely true actually. I am going to help myself. I've accepted the fact that I'm a bit boring.

Deidre looks at him

All right, very boring. But I've decided to make a conscious effort to do something about it.

Deidre I hope you're not doing it for me.

Derek Oh no, I'm doing it for myself.

Deidre How are you going to go about it?

Derek Teddy's going to take me under his wing. He's taking me to this club he goes to in Cardiff.

Deidre So when are you going to start?

Derek Right now—tonight.

Nick (*calling over*) Derek? Drink?

Derek (*attempting confidence*) Yes, I'll have another glass.

He looks at Deidre before he joins Nick at the table. His attempt at confidence has made him walk funny. As he walks over to Nick he's not doing a bad imitation of John Wayne

Derek takes his drink and turns to the others

(*Calling for attention*) Listen, everyone. (*He puts one hand in his pocket and holds his drink with the other*) Heard a little yarn the other day.

Deidre moves away to sit on the settee, but the others listen to him

There were these two hippos . . . Connie and Bronnie. They both put on some make-up and went to a dance. When they got there, Ronnie—

Joyce Who's Ronnie?

Derek One of the hippos.

Pearl They were Connie and Bronnie.

Derek Were they? Oh right—Connie and Bronnie then. When they got there, Connie took a shine to this other hippo who was already up on the floor dancing. She waited all night for him to come over and ask her for a dance, but he never did. Eventually Bronnie decided that if he wasn't going to ask her to dance, she was going to ask him.

Deidre I thought it was Connie who wanted to dance with him?

Derek It was.

Deidre Well you said Bronnie.

Derek Well, it was Connie. I think. Yes, it was Connie. She went over to him and tapped in. So anyway— they were both there—dancing, and after a minute he said to her, "What's your name?" and she said "Ronnie".

Joyce (*correcting him*) Connie.

Derek That's right, Connie. And she said to him, "What's yours?" And he said . . . (*He thinks about it*) Brian. And with that she fainted on the floor. Bronnie rushed over to her and brought her round and said, "What the

hell's the matter with you?" And Connie said, "Oh, I couldn't help it—
I've never danced with Brian Hippo before."

*No one laughs. Derek laughs helplessly, then realizes no one has joined him
and stops immediately*

Well, Teddy thought it was funny.

Roz enters

Roz (*coming out of the house*) I knew I shouldn't have let him touch
anything.
Nick What's the matter?
Roz That Eddie chap has messed about with our television aerial and we
haven't got a picture at all now.
Deidre It's my fault. I should never have brought him.
Derek (*still feeling his feet*) Shall I ask him to leave?
Joyce Leave him alone. With a bit of luck he might blow himself up.

Teddy comes out of the house, still holding his trousers up

Teddy I hope you haven't started without me?
Joyce No, you're all right Ted. He hasn't spilt the beans yet.
Teddy Well before you do, will you do me a favour, Nick?
Nick What is it?
Teddy Do me up?

*Nick does up Teddy's fly and top button. Teddy watches him all the while.
When Nick finishes he looks up at Teddy who is already looking at him. Teddy
does a very slow wink. Nick hastily moves away, embarrassed, talking as he
does so*

Nick Right ... well it's about time I think to, er ...
Joyce Announce ...
Nick The next ...
Teddy Show.
Nick Yes.

*Everyone seems to take up a position. Joyce, Mona and Teddy sit, in that
order, on the bench. Nick is standing* CS

Teddy No long speeches now, Nick.
Joyce No, just sock it to us.
Nick Well ... before I tell you what it is—I must make one point clear.
Teddy Oh, here we go.
Nick Some of you will be—
Teddy Pleased.
Nick And some of you will be—
Joyce Disappointed.
Teddy (*to Joyce*) He says the same thing every year.
Nick What I want you to remember is this. You want to do a particular
show for what's in it for *you*. I choose a show for what's in it for the
society. After deliberating over it for some time—

Teddy mocks a snore. Joyce nudges him and he "awakens"

Teddy Oh I'm sorry—has he announced it? What is it—*Phantom*?
Mona (*disgusted*) Shut up, Teddy.

Teddy and Joyce pull a funny face. He considers himself told off

Nick I'm pleased to announce that our next production is——

Everyone sits bolt upright

   Sweet Charity.

There is a deadly silence. Teddy and Mona are gobsmacked

   For those of you that don't know it—it's a very popular show.
Pearl Not with this crowd, it's not.
Nick And you'll be glad to know, Pearl, that it's quite successful at the box office.

There is another terrible silence. Suddenly there is a strange whooping noise. Joyce starts to cry hysterically. Teddy tries to comfort her. Roz crosses the stage, passing Nick, to join them

Roz (*to Nick*) I'll never forgive you for this.

Joyce is by now uncontrollable. Teddy and Roz get her to her feet and try to take her indoors. Teddy lets go of Joyce as they reach the patio doors. He is not going inside

Roz (*to Teddy*) I don't know what to do with her.
Teddy Try and calm her down.
Roz How will I do that?
Teddy Give her a black and green or something.

   Roz takes Joyce into the house

Joyce's cries die down after a moment or two. There is complete silence on the patio. Teddy turns now to face Nick

   (*Placing his hands on his hips*) Well!!!
Nick Is that all, Teddy? I imagined you'd have more to say than that.
Teddy (*advancing towards him*) Oh, I have, luv—you take it from me!
Nick Well now's the time to air your views, before I announce the cast.
Teddy Well for starters . . . as soon as I get these off my fingers. (*He holds up his hands*) I'll be ringing the warden in Garth Wen and I'll be making arrangements to have your mother ousted. (*He gestures with one of his thumbs*)
Nick Now, Teddy, we mustn't get personal about all this.
Teddy Hey listen, luv, it's your mother who's getting personal, not me.
Nick I know you had your mind set on another show, but my hands are tied.
Teddy I don't want to know if you're into bondage.
Derek (*really pleased, and forgetting himself*) Tell him who's playing Charity.

He realizes immediately what he has said and stiffens. Deidre smells a rat

Nick (*jumping in, hoping to save the situation*) Well, I think I had a stroke of genius when I thought of this.

Mona (*standing, indicating Derek*) How does he know?

Nick What?

Mona Who's playing Charity.

Derek (*lying through his teeth*) Er . . . I don't.

Teddy (*equally suspicious*) But you said—

Deidre "Tell him who's playing Charity"—

Teddy As if you already knew.

Derek (*deciding to come clean*) That's right . . . I do.

Mona (*she is outraged*) But Nick doesn't tell anyone.

Nick I asked his advice. (*To Derek*) Didn't I?

Derek Er . . . that's right.

Teddy (*to Nick*) What does he know about casting a show?

Nick I wanted to get an unbiased opinion.

Teddy Well, why didn't you ask me then?

Deidre So who *is* playing Charity?

Derek is really in a spot and can't get out of it

Teddy (*to Nick*) Yes, come on . . . spill the beans.

Nick Well I've found the most perfect Charity. With her dedication and my direction, she's going to be wonderful.

Teddy Well, who is she?

Nick She's not a million miles away from here.

He is looking at Deidre. Deidre sees this, checks behind her, then realizes what's going on

Deidre You're not serious!

Teddy (*to Nick, after a quick look at Deidre; screaming the word*) *Her*?!

Nick (*smiling at Deidre*) Will you do it for me, Deidre?

Deidre (*making a bee-line for Derek*) You must think I'm stupid.

She pushes Nick out of the way

(*To Derek*) I know you're behind all this.

Derek No, I'm not.

Deidre (*pushing Derek* DR *of the settee*) What are you trying to do? Make a fool of me?

Derek I'd never do that.

Deidre (*shouting*) Just because I said I'd like to play Charity a couple of times it doesn't mean I'd like to play it.

Derek Doesn't it?

Deidre What the hell do you think you're trying to do?

Derek Please you.

Deidre By putting me on the stage?

Derek I thought that's what you wanted.

Deidre (*shouting even louder*) All I want is for you to get out of my life. For good!

Nick Don't take it all out on him.

Deidre Oh, I'm not. I haven't said what I think of you, yet.

Mona (*advancing towards Nick but addressing Deidre*) You're going to have to join the queue.

Teddy (*to Mona*) And you're going to have to get behind *me*, luv!

Pearl Don't all pick on him.

The following speeches by Deidre, Mona, Teddy, Pearl and Jessica should be run simultaneously

During this hub-bub Derek looks and sees the aerial on the table. He picks it up and eventually decides to ascend the ladder, which is still propped against the side of the house

When Derek is about half-way up the ladder, the Lights should come down and the quarrelling should fade

Deidre I'll do more than pick on him—fancy scheming behind my back. And don't try and tell me it'll be a marvellous opportunity. I don't know why yet, but you're not doing all this for me. There must be a hell of a lot in it for yourself. For some reason, you and him have plotted this between you. I thought I meant more to you as a friend, but I can see I was wrong. Some friend, to let me go up on the stage and make a fool of myself. And don't tell me you won't allow that to happen because if you can do it to your own sister-in-law, you can do it to me. It's not a bit of wonder she's turned out like she has—and the pity of it she's all ready and set to let you do it to her again. Well that's fine by me—get her to play Charity—she'll jump at it—and if she won't do it you're just going to have to find some other sucker who will. And while you're at it, see if you can find a prompt at the same time!

Mona You've done some dirty tricks in your time, Nick. Do you have any idea what an honour and a challenge *West Side Story* would have been for you, let alone me? I can't say that I'm not disappointed, because I am. I'm disappointed in you too, as a person. Many people have thought you a rat, but I've always said "speak as you find". And by and large I've always found you more or less straight. I know we haven't always seen eye-to-eye over various things, but it has always been for the good of the show. It's always the show that's kept us together—but not anymore— this is the beginning of the end as far as I'm concerned. And far be it from me to speak ill of anyone, but as it is, I'm forced to agree with half the chorus in our society when they refer to you as the pig you obviously are!

Teddy Yes . . . a fine friend you turned out to be. I never thought you'd end up doing something like this to me. Me—who's given the best years of my life to this society. You've had it with me, Nick. I've done my lot for you . . . and your mother come to that. I told you how important *Oklahoma* is to me—you know I had my heart set on it and you more or less promised it to me, and what did you do? Go behind my back like the sly fox you are!

Pearl I think you're all being awfully unfair. Like Nick said, he's only doing it for the good of the society. It's all very well for you all to want something different, but at the end of the day, we've got to be practical. I don't know the show myself, but I'm sure it's an excellent choice. Why don't you all stop thinking about yourselves and start thinking about the show and how to get the society back on it's feet? And talking of feet (*to Mona*), you ought to be behind Nick all the way, being a member of the production team. (*To Deidre*) And there's no need for the fuss you're making, either. Many would jump at the chance of playing the lead in a musical. And Teddy, I thought you had more feeling. I think you're all a bunch of ungrateful little ... If I had my way, the only thing I'd cast you all in is a boat out to sea!

Jessica Thank you very much! How many more lies have you told me? *Gigi*, he says, you'll be marvellous—the talk of the place. You knew all along you wouldn't be doing it. You only said it to have your own way with me. Used me—that's all you've done. Well, don't think you're going to get away with it—because you're not. You haven't heard the last of this. You're a skunk, that's what you are. Others told me but I couldn't see it. I didn't want to see it but I do now. What hurts the most is how easily I believed you. You must have thought I was a pushover. Well, you'll soon see who's going to get pushed. You'll curse the day you ever put a hand on me. By the time I've finished with you you'll be begging me to play *Gigi*—and do you know what I'll tell you then? Up your fat arse!

It is possible that the above speeches may not be needed in their entirety. As soon as Derek has begun to ascend the ladder, the Lights can fade and so too may the chaos

SCENE 2

Ten minutes later

The Lights come up to reveal Teddy, Pearl, Mona, Deidre and Jessica on stage. Teddy is sitting DR *on the garden bench; Pearl is perched on the arm of the bench on the side opposite Teddy, Mona, Deidre and Jessica occupy chairs at various points on the patio, as far away from each other as possible*

We hear the sounds of a row off, between Nick and Roz, accompanied by Joyce's sobbing

Nick (*off*) You're not being at all reasonable.
Roz (*off*) You promised!
Nick (*off*) I didn't.
Roz (*off*) Do you have any idea what sort of effect this could have on Joyce?
Nick (*off*) Don't threaten me.
Roz (*off*) I'm not, but if she does something silly it'll be your fault.
Nick (*off*) You're not being fair!
Roz (*off, screaming*) *I'm* not being fair? Look at her—look at Joyce ... she's a wreck.
Nick (*off*) She was like that before I announced the show.

Joyce breaks down even more after Nick's remark

Roz (*off, to Nick*) *Now* look what you've done.
Nick (*off*) She can cry and scream as much as she likes, Roz, there's no way she could play Charity!

Joyce's sobs grow louder

Roz (*off, to Nick*) Oh, bugger off!
Joyce (*off, screaming through her tears*) Yes, bugger off!

Pause

> *Nick comes out of the house on to the patio*

He looks around. No one turns to look at him. He senses an atmosphere

Nick (*trying to be chirpy*) Everything all right out here?

No one answers

> Good.

Pause

Nick sees that the ladder is still propped up against the house. He goes to take it down

> Can someone give me a hand?

The others turn to look at him, then look away

> Not you Teddy. I know you can't.

Teddy (*sharply*) I wasn't going to anyway, luv!

Pause

Nick It won't take long. Two minutes. (*He pauses*) Mona?

No answer

> I see. (*He goes to the ladder, attempts to take it down himself*)

Pearl (*after watching him struggle*) I'll help you, Nick.
Teddy Traitor!

Pearl and Nick take the ladder down

> *Pearl and Nick exit with the ladder*

Another terrible silence

Mona I wish someone would say something.

No one does

> Deidre? (*Mona sighs*) Teddy?

Teddy What can I say? I'm devastated. That's the only word I can think of—devastated.
Mona I wonder what will happen now?
Teddy The show, you mean?
Mona Well, of course. As I see it, he has three options. He could cast

someone else—he could change the show—or he could ask Deidre to do it.

Deidre He won't be getting me on any stage.

Jessica Well, if you ask me—

Teddy (*jumping in*) We're not, luv, right? No bugger's asking you anything!

Jessica I think he'll change the show.

Mona To what?

Teddy You can forget *Gigi*—that was a pipe dream.

Mona A bribe.

Teddy I think he'll dig his heels in. I reckon he'll do *Charity* now even if it kills him.

Mona And if the show doesn't kill him, maybe someone will!

Teddy (*sitting upright on the bench*) Hey, it would make a bloody marvellous Agatha Christie, wouldn't it? You've heard of *Murder at the Vicarage*? This would be *Murder on the Patio*. I can see it all now. We'd all be called indoors for some reason—all, that is, except Nick, who'd stayed out here to try and light the barbecue. We weren't inside more than five minutes—when we returned, there he was, "slumped" over the barbecue, "dead".

Mona Burnt to a cinder!

Teddy No—don't be silly, he couldn't light the bloody thing. No—he'd been stabbed in the chest—but it wasn't that that killed him. A post-mortem later revealed that the murderer had shoved a copy of the next production up his arse. We all had a motive. The only clue Nick left was a scribbled message he managed to write in his own blood on a patio slab. The message read . . . let me think now. Yes. "Why! Why! I'll get you for this, you baa . . . oooohhhh!".

Everyone falls about laughing, Teddy hardest

Deidre That's an awful long message.

Teddy (*hysterical*) He'd lost a lot of blood.

Everyone laughs again

   Nick and Pearl enter back on to the patio

Nick (*pleased that everything seems to be fine now*) Having a good time then?

The laughing stops immediately

   Good, that's what I like to hear.

There is a pause

   Right, let's try something on the barbecue. (*He goes to it and busies himself*) Let me see . . . burgers, sausage. (*He holds one up and shows it to Teddy*) Do you fancy a sausage, Teddy?

Teddy (*turning round and seeing him*) Oh, very bloody funny.

Nick I'll put a couple on anyway.

Nick cooks on the barbecue

There is another pause. Eventually Teddy looks over in Deidre's direction—she nods and throws a look towards Nick. Teddy gets the message and pipes up

Teddy Well, we all want to know, but it looks like I'm the mouthpiece. What's going to happen now?

Nick doesn't answer

Nick! I'm talking to you.

Nick Sorry?

Teddy What's going to happen now?

Nick With the show, you mean?

Teddy What else?

Nick Nothing, as far as I know.

Jessica You're still going ahead then?

Teddy And sticking to your guns?

Nick Of course.

Teddy (*to the others*) Didn't I tell you? Didn't I say that's what would happen?

Nick Perhaps I'll hold auditions.

Teddy Ooh, hey, now do you think that's wise? We'll have all the bloody riff-raff in.

Nick What else can I do? The lady of my choice isn't interested.

Deidre I don't believe for one minute that I was your choice. I haven't got to the bottom of it yet, but Derek's involved with it somewhere. Come to think of it, I haven't seen him for a while. Where is he?

Mona Perhaps he's gone home.

Derek (*off*) No I haven't.

Everyone looks at one another

(*Off*) I'm up here!

Everyone looks around the patio

(*Off*) Up here!

They all turn their backs to the audience and face the house. Derek is up on the roof, out of sight of the audience

Nick Derek, what the hell do you think you're doing?

Derek (*off*) I'm going to jump.

Pause

I'm going to do it.

Teddy (*turning to Deidre*) Deidre, do something.

Deidre Like what?

Teddy Well, talk him down or something.

Deidre He hasn't got the guts. I'd call his bluff. (*Calling to Derek*) Aye, go on . . . jump if you want to.

Teddy No, no . . . (*Calling to Derek*) Derek? This is Teddy. I'm going to get a ladder, luv.

Derek (*off, shouting*) No! You leave it where it is.

Nick Derek, what's the point in all this?

Derek (*off*) I don't want to go on anymore. I still love Deidre and I can't face Monday.

Nick If you jump you're only going to break a couple of bones. You won't kill yourself from that height.

Derek (*off*) I'll only come down if Deidre'll come back to me.

Deidre (*calling*) Never! (*She goes and sits down on the settee*)

Derek (*off*) Right, that's it. Out of the way, I'm going to do it.

Teddy (*panicking*) No, no, Derek. Listen now. Derek, are you listening to me? What's wrong between you and Deidre won't be put right by a jump. (*To the others*) Well it won't will it?

Eddie comes out of the house

Eddie Now who's gone and moved that aerial?

Nick (*pointing to Derek*) He's got it up there.

Eddie (*joining the others to look up*) Oh, aye? Hey, do me a favour, butt. See that aerial you've got in your hand—can you hold it about six inches to the left? No, no, you haven't got to take it out of its socket.

Pause

What are you doing now?

Pause

No! It's no good swinging it around like that!

Suddenly the aerial comes crashing down on to the patio. Everyone scatters

(*Looking at everyone*) Hey, there's something bloody funny about him.

Nick picks up the aerial

Teddy (*to Deidre*) I think he's flipped.

Eddie (*to Nick*) Give it to me. (*Taking it*) It's all right, it's not damaged. Maybe I can fix it to the mantelpiece. (*He starts to go back inside the house, muttering to himself as he goes*) Or on the window sill. Perhaps I can make a feature out of it. Something multi-purpose like a coat hanger or a letter rack or something.

Eddie exits, everyone watching him go

Nick This is getting to be a nightmare.

Mona And none of us have woken up yet.

Derek (*off, shouting*) Are you ready—here I go!

At this point Roz rushes out on to the patio

Roz (*seething, to Nick*) You ... bastard! (*She is holding Jessica's dress, which is covered in paint*)

Nick Roz!

Roz Don't you "Roz" me.

Nick What's the matter?

Roz (*throwing the dress at him*) Try and explain that one!

Nick What are you talking about?

Roz Didn't think I'd find it in there, did you?

Nick Find what?

Roz That dress—in the cane trunk in the spare room.

Nick I didn't know it was there.

Roz I'm sure. If I hadn't had the idea to get Joyce to audition for you, you might just have got away with it.

Nick With what?

Roz It's covered in bloody paint! The stripes on that dress are going the same way as yours. I might be a lot of things, Nick, but I'm nobody's fool.

Nick I didn't put it in the trunk—Mona did. (*To Mona*) Didn't you?

Mona (*smiling sweetly*) I don't know what you're talking about.

Roz Why would Mona put the dress there?

Mona Exactly.

Nick (*on the spot*) Look, you don't honestly think there's anything between Jessica and me?

Roz I know there's a wet bench in the garage and the only ones to have paint on them are you and that little slut!

Nick (*to Jessica*) Tell her she's got it all wrong. Explain to her—go on.

There is a pause

Roz Well, I'm waiting.

Jessica He's been after me for months—but I won't have anything to do with him. He's tried every trick in the book. He even promised to do *Gigi* for me.

Nick No. (*To Roz*) Look ... it wasn't like that.

Roz storms off into the house

Teddy (*to Nick*) Ooohhh, you rat!

Nick (*to Jessica*) Thank you very much.

Jessica Don't mention it.

Pearl Go after her, Nick. I don't like to see her upset like that.

Nick She'll be all right.

Pearl I wouldn't be so sure. If you don't sort things out, you're going to end up another Derek and Deidre.

Teddy Speaking of which, we haven't heard anything from Superman for a bit.

Deidre (*unconcernedly*) He's still up there, I've no doubt.

Mona (*looking up*) He's not, you know.

Teddy What?

Mona He's not there—he's gone.

Teddy Well, he can't have gone far ... where is he?

They are now all looking up at the roof again

Teddy	
Mona	
Deidre	(*together, shouting*) Derek! Derek!
Nick	
Pearl	
Jessica	

There is a garbled scream from Derek as he jumps off the roof on the other side of the house

Teddy (*panicking*) Oh my God, he's done it!

Suddenly there is pandemonium

Nick, Pearl and Mona rush off to go to Derek

Teddy is about to join them, then realizes he'd be no help

Teddy No, what am I doing? It's pointless me going ... what can I do?

Deidre hasn't moved. She has her back to the audience but faces Teddy

(*Looking at Deidre, very dramatically*) Der ... you're a cold fish, Deidre.

Deidre's reaction isn't the way Teddy reads it. She is concerned and almost upset by the situation

Deidre I couldn't go. I couldn't face him. Go and see if he's all right, Teddy. I don't want anything to happen to him.

Joyce appears at the patio doors

Joyce steps outside. She is still very emotional and still very drunk

Joyce I ... want ... to ... go ... home.

Teddy Hang on Deidre, let me sort Joyce out first. (*Taking Joyce back indoors*) Come on, luv. Come back in and have a lie-down.

Teddy and Joyce go inside

There is a pause

Jessica Do you think he's all right?

Deidre looks at her

The boring old fart.

Deidre Let me tell you something. That man's got more heart than you'll ever have.

Jessica Who needs heart these days, luv?

Deidre We all do!

Jessica Then why'd you leave him?

Pause

Deidre Is it true about you and Nick?

Jessica It's true he fancies me something rotten, yeah. It's true that he promised me *Gigi*.

Deidre It's upset Roz.

Jessica Serves him right.

Pause

Deidre So what happened to the dress?

Jessica What happened to the dress is exactly what Roz thinks happened. I started wandering around the house, you know—having a look ...

suddenly I was in the garage. Nick found me in there and we had a bit on a bench.

Deidre Sex?

Jessica Na ... just heavy petting, really.

Deidre How could you?

Jessica Well, he promised me a show, didn't he? I'm glad I didn't go all the way now, though.

Deidre You'd wreck a marriage for a lead in a musical?

Jessica (*nodding*) Pretty lousy reason, isn't it?

Deidre Is there ever a good one?

Jessica You tell me, luv.

Deidre smiles but doesn't answer

There are sounds of confusion coming from inside the house

> *Teddy comes out on to the patio*

Teddy (*coming towards Deidre*) It's all over, Deid' ... he's down.

Deidre Is he all right?

Teddy He's done something to his leg—but he'll live. They're trying to get him on the settee but Joyce is lying on it and she won't budge. It's bedlam in there. That Eddie chap has got the guts of the TV and video spread all over the lounge carpet. He won't get the video to work now cause I've gone and stepped on the heads.

Deidre But Derek's going to be all right?

Teddy Well, perhaps you'd better have a look at him—you'd have more of an idea than me.

Deidre You're right.

> *Derek is brought out on to the patio by Nick and Mona*

Derek keeps his right foot off the ground

Nick (*to Deidre and Teddy*) He insisted on coming out here.

Derek Yes—I've been enough trouble.

Teddy (*indicating the bench*) Put him down here.

Nick puts Derek on the bench, then moves around the patio, coming to stand just DL in front of the settee

> *Pearl comes out on to the patio*

Derek I'm sorry Deidre—everyone. I'm terribly sorry. It was a silly thing to do, wasn't it?

Deidre How's your leg?

Derek Painful.

Deidre Let me check—make sure you haven't broken anything. (*She takes off his shoe and sock, then rolls up his trouser leg*)

Derek I'm all in one piece ... except my heart.

Deidre ignores this remark

Teddy has been watching Nick. After a pause he moves to him

Teddy I didn't see Roz in there, Nick.

Nick Probably cooling off somewhere. She'll be all right.

Teddy Listen Nick. (*He takes his arm and moves him even further* DL) The more I think about it the more I'm coming around to the idea.

Nick What are you talking about?

Teddy *Sweet Charity*. Nice show really. Oscar is never a part I saw myself in, but I will do it for you.

Nick Why do you think you never saw yourself playing Oscar?

Teddy I don't know. It just never appealed to me.

Nick And do you know why?

Teddy shakes his head

Because you're not right for it.

Teddy I haven't been right for a lot of parts, but I've still done 'em.

Nick If I gave you Oscar it would be a disaster—and you know as well as I do that the company couldn't take another one.

Teddy (*giving in*) What do you want me to play for you then?

Pause

Nick Nothing.

Pause

Teddy Nothing?

Nick I'm going to ask Nicholas Rees to do it.

Teddy (*exploding*) Nicholas Rees? (*He can't find the words*) He's got a north eye. You're not serious? Didn't you see him in *Fiddler*? He was bloody awful. (*Suddenly becoming very hurt*) Well ... To think you've chosen him over me.

Nick It's nothing personal.

Teddy (*almost crying*) Tell me now then—just the two of us—it won't go any further. Why haven't you cast me?

Nick I'll never give in to blackmail.

Teddy (*outraged*) I've never blackmailed you.

Nick Oh, come on now.

Teddy (*insisting*) I haven't. I might have put a bit of pressure on from time to time—but from what I can see every bugger here has done that.

Nick I don't know why you're getting so upset. At least you can go and play Schubert now.

Teddy (*screaming*) They haven't bloody *asked* me. And if they had you wouldn't see my arse for dust, believe me. (*He is getting quite hysterical now*) You'll be sorry you've done this, Nick. I've given the best years of my life to this society—and now you've done this to me. Well, this is war as far as I'm concerned. Love me and I'm a pussy-cat ... cross me and I'm a bloody tiger. (*He turns to leave*) I'm going home ... I'm a bag of nerves. (*Turning back to face Nick*) I've done my lot for you, Nick—and for your mother come to that! You don't want to think that doing *Sweet Charity* is going to solve a lot of problems because believe me, your problems are just beginning. (*He turns to the others as he moves to a position just* R *of the* *patio doors. He holds his arms out)* Look what he's doing to me ... I'm a bath of sweat. (*He wipes his forehead with the back of his hand. Then turns viciously and points to Nick)* You forget, see, that I've got friends in low places. I've got a contact in *The Rhondda Leader*. And just imagine your embarrassment when I give them the story of your mother, and the little business she's started up at the age of sixty-eight! Imagine *that* splashed across the front page. No ... no forget about *The Rhondda Leader*—think big, Teddy ... think big. I'm going to go straight to *The News of the World*!

Teddy exits

His outburst has got the attention of everyone on stage

Pearl comes to the patio doors in time to watch him make his exit

There is an embarrassing pause while everyone looks at Nick

Nick A drink, anyone?
Deidre (*to Derek; indicating his foot*) I don't like the look of this.
Mona Hell hath no fury ...
Nick When are people going to realize that they're not going to have their own way with me.
Jessica Yeah, I'd like to know the answer to that one, too.
Pearl Nick, I don't want to worry you, but Roz is in the bedroom ... packing.
Nick Nothing to worry about.
Pearl She's very hurt.
Nick She'll come round. She'll probably spend a couple of days at her mother's then things will be okay.
Deidre (*to Derek*) I think you should go to the hospital.
Derek No, I don't want to do that.
Nick What's the verdict?
Deidre His ankle is badly swollen. I think he should take a trip to the hospital. He says it's painful. He might have broken a small bone or something.
Nick There you are then, Derek, better take the advice of the expert.
Deidre I'm hardly that.
Pearl Shall I ring for an ambulance?
Nick No need for that. Someone will take him in the car.

Mona and Deidre look at each other

I'd take him myself, but things being as they are with Roz, I think it's better if I stay here and play host.
Mona (*to Nick*) Well who's going to take him?

Slight pause. She looks at Deidre who doesn't offer

Then I suppose it will have to be me. Will you come with me as well, Pearl? Two of us should handle him all right.

Pearl and Mona get Derek to his feet (or foot). They move towards the patio door

Deidre No wait! Perhaps I'd better take him.
Mona Are you sure? I don't mind doing it, really.
Deidre It's all right. (*To Derek*) Give me your arm.

He does, and beams over at Nick

It's all right Pearl—I'll manage him now.
Pearl Do you want us to come with you?
Derek (*insisting*) No ... no, we'll be fine. Goodnight all. (*He walks off on both feet, with his arm firmly around Deidre's shoulder*)

Derek and Deidre exit, the others watching them go

Mona Well, I never expected that.
Pearl I wonder if it will come to anything.
Mona What a night!
Jessica (*threateningly*) And it's not over yet!

Pause

Nick Shall I tell you something? I'm not the big horrible person you all think I am.
Jessica Aren't you?
Nick I changed the show to *Sweet Charity* because I didn't realize until tonight how little money we had.
Mona How do we know that's true?
Pearl I can vouch for that. I've been trying to tell him for days about the problem.
Jessica What difference does *Sweet Charity* make as opposed to another show?
Nick Derek offered to put up the money.
Mona (*putting the pieces together*) As long as Deidre played the lead.
Nick You've got it. Ten thousand pounds is a lot of money. Under the circumstances, I couldn't afford to refuse.
Jessica (*amazed*) Ten thousand pounds? I don't believe you.

Nick takes the cheque from his shirt pocket and gives it to Jessica

Nick I couldn't say anything because Derek asked me not to.
Mona Why are you telling us now?
Nick Nothing to lose any more. He'll probably want the cheque back.

Jessica gives the cheque back to Nick

Pearl What will you do if he does?
Nick No idea.
Mona And if he doesn't—will you still do *Charity*?
Nick It all rather depends on Derek, doesn't it?
Pearl If you do get to go ahead with *Charity*, who will you cast?
Nick That's the least of my problems at the moment.

Mona I bet you've got someone in mind.

Nick (*shaking his head*) No, I haven't. I said earlier on, if we do go ahead I'll probably hold auditions.

Jessica (*to Nick*) I want to ask you something.

He looks at her

What was the show going to be?

Mona Yes, I'd like to know that too.

Nick (*looking from Mona to Jessica*) *Gigi*. That's why I was painting the benches.

Roz comes out of the house carrying a suitcase

She heads straight for Nick and sets it down at his feet

Nick Now what's all this?

Roz What's all what?

Nick Look, I think it's all a bit pointless.

Roz What is?

Nick You—trotting off back to your mother's.

Roz What are you talking about?

Nick You've packed a case.

Roz Yes—but for you, not me.

Nick What?

Roz I'm not going anywhere, Nick. You're the one who's done the dirty.

Nick I haven't done anything.

Jessica (*to Roz*) That's true—he hasn't. I let you think he had because I wanted to get him back for not doing *Gigi*.

A slight pause

Pearl (*looking at her watch*) Look, it's ten to ten. There's not much of the night left. Let's throw a couple of things on the barbecue and finish it off properly.

Pearl, Mona and Jessica go to the barbecue, leaving Nick and Roz alone

Nick What do you say?

Roz Things can't be washed over as easily as that.

Pause

Nick If I have to leave, where will I go?

Roz I don't know. Back to your mother, I suppose.

Nick If what Teddy said is true, there's not going to be any room for me.

Roz Where is he, anyway?

Nick Gone. His huff arrived and he departed in it.

Mona You've upset him?

Nick I've probably upset everyone.

Roz What about Derek? And Deidre's not here either.

Nick Both gone off to hospital.

Roz Pearl told me what happened.

Pause

Nick How's Joyce?

Roz She took it very badly.

Nick I had a good reason for doing what I did.

Roz She's desperately trying to get her confidence back.

Nick She's not going to get it back while she's still on the bottle.

Roz It's crazy I know, but that's the only time she's got any confidence—when she's had a few.

Nick What if I gave her another part and she screwed up? She almost committed suicide after the last show.

Roz She wouldn't let you down again. She wouldn't let herself down.

Nick I couldn't take the chance.

Roz Let her audition for you. You know there isn't a part she couldn't play.

Nick She couldn't play any part sober.

Roz Please?

Nick (*sighing*) I don't know. I'm under all sorts of pressure at the moment.

Roz Like what?

Nick Well, Teddy's got it in for me. He's making all kinds of threats . . . I'm not sure what's going to come of it. He left in a bath of perspiration.

Roz Joyce is my sister, Nick, and blood is thicker than sweat. If you won't do anything else, do this for me.

Nick She's an alcoholic.

Roz No, she's not. She's just got a bit of a drink problem, that's all.

    At this point Joyce comes out

She stands just outside the patio doors. She is still very much drunk, and is carrying a top hat and cane

Roz sees her. Joyce and Roz wink at each other

    Let her audition for you. Give her a chance to prove herself. If you don't think she's right for *Charity* after that—I won't say any more about it.

Before Nick has a chance to answer, Joyce starts to sing "If they could see me now"

The others look on in amazement. During the first verse she moves all over the place . . . trying desperately to strut her stuff. Because she is so inebriated, she is not doing a very good job

Black-out as she reaches the end of the verse

In the darkness an orchestra is heard playing the intro to the same song. A huge shimmer curtain comes down, completely blocking out the patio. A spotlight hits the centre of the curtain, and Charity steps through the curtain and into the light. She has a bobbed wig, high heels, fishnet tights and a black body-stocking with a sparkling silver jacket. She turns to face the audience and begins to sing the remaining two verses of the song, accompanied by the music

    Charity is in fact being played by Teddy. Big finish to the song

              BLACK-OUT

FURNITURE AND PROPERTY LIST

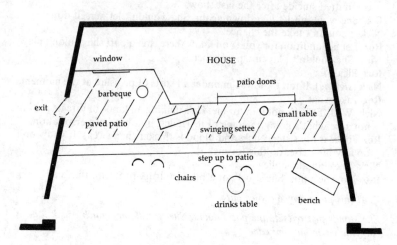

window HOUSE

patio doors

barbeque

exit

paved patio

small table

swinging settee

step up to patio

chairs

drinks table

bench

ACT I

Scene 1

On stage: Bench
Chairs
Drinks table. *On it:* bottles of liquor, punch bowl, ice, glasses, lemon, etc.
Also an ash-tray
Barbecue. *On it:* charcoal
Smaller table
Swinging settee

Off stage: Gallon can **(Pearl)**

Personal: **Derek:** cheque book and pen
Nick: fire-lighter, matches, car keys, watch
Teddy: cigarettes, matches, apron
Pearl: watch, handbag (with bills in)
Eddie: copy of *TV Times*, wrist-watch "TV"

ACT II

SCENE 1

Set: Barbecue UL
             makings for a salad roll (*on small table* UR)

Off stage: Television set **(Eddie)**
             Double ladders **(Eddie)**
             TV aerial **(Eddie)**

SCENE 2

Set: Barbecue in its original position (*just* L *of* CS)

Off stage: TV aerial **(Derek)**
             Jessica's dress **(Roz)**
             Suitcase **(Roz)**
             Top hat and cane **(Joyce)**

LIGHTING PLOT

Exterior. A garden/patio area. The same scene throughout

ACT I, SCENE 1.   Early evening

To open: Summer evening sunshine

Cue 1   **Mona** smiles as she turns to face the audience   (Page 35)
         Black-out

ACT II, SCENE 1.   An hour or so later

To open: Exterior lighting: summer evening sunshine

Cue 2   **Derek** is about half-way up the ladder   (Page 61)
         Fade to black-out

ACT II, SCENE 2.   Ten minutes later

To open: Exterior lighting: summer evening sunshine

Cue 3   As **Joyce** reaches the end of the verse   (Page 73)
         Black-out. When ready bring up spotlight on centre of curtain

Cue 4   Big finish to **Teddy**'s rendition of "If They Could See Me Now"   (Page 73)
         Black-out

EFFECTS PLOT

ACT I

Cue 1   **Deidre** laughs   (Page 34)
Smoke begins to pour out of the kitchen window

Cue 2   **Deidre:** "I was forced into it."   (Page 34)
Smoke billows out of the patio doors

ACT II

Cue 3   **Nick:** "I'll put a couple on anyway."   (Page 63)
Barbecue effect (burning coals, smoking meat)

Cue 4   Black-out as **Joyce** reaches the end of the verse   (Page 73)
An orchestra is heard playing "If They Could See Me Now"